ROMAN TOWNS IN BRITAIN

Alan Sorrell

ROMAN TOWNS IN BRITAIN

Foreword by Dr Graham Webster

B T BATSFORD LTD LONDON

First published 1976

© Elizabeth Sorrell, 1976

ISBN 0 1734 3237 3

Filmset by Keyspools Ltd, Golborne and
printed in Great Britain by Butler and Tanner Ltd, Frome

for the publishers
B. T. Batsford Ltd, 4 Fitzhardinge Street, London W1H 0AH

Contents

The Illustrations

Foreword by Dr Graham Webster

The manuscript was passed to me in an incomplete state, but, judging from the drawings which Alan Sorrell had selected and the passages on London and Lincoln which were in early draft, he intended adding sections on Caerwent and the civil settlements attached to the forts, like those as Housesteads and Corbridge, which he mentioned in his general chapter. I have added these missing parts, and also revised those passages in early draft in a style which I hope he would have approved. His own text he would no doubt have checked and asked others to read. It has been my aim to retain as much of the original as possible, although in some instances not wholly accepting his views, but I have corrected or deleted where the facts were inaccurate. In most cases this was not the fault of Alan Sorrell, since he could not possibly have had all the evidence from recent unpublished excavations, and reassessments which follow.

This gives me an opportunity of adding my own tribute to a man who did more than he realised to further interest in Roman Britain. He was a most painstaking artist and insisted always on getting all the details as near to the truth as possible. Any mistakes must be where he was misled or where later discoveries show somewhat different structures. His fine lively drawings have been a delight to a whole generation of readers (young and old alike), and he has given flesh and blood to the dull dry bones of archaeological reports, which are often written in such an obscure way as to repel the interested enquirer. He little realised his effect on the professional, but, by his insistence on reconstruction, he forced us to think about the appearance of the buildings we were excavating. It was a bracing and salutory experience. I for one can date a number of new ideas about Wroxeter from the time of his visit. Here was a mind and a hand which demanded answers which had to be reasonable and strictly in accordance with the known evidence. His quite firm, but persistent, pressure on people who are notoriously awkward and argumentative, produced the remarkable results we admire so much in this book, and that in itself was a major triumph for Alan Sorrell.

Acknowledgements

The Publishers wish to thank the following for permission to reproduce the reconstructions and photographs appearing in this book.

Bath City Council for page 70; the Trustees of the British Museum for pages 11 and 13; City of London Police for pages 22–3 and 32–3; Castle Museum, Colchester for page 46; Colchester and Essex Museum for pages 45 and 48–9; Department of the Environment for pages 55, 58, 66, 76 and 77; Guildhall Museum, London, for pages 24, 26, 27, 30, 31 and 34; *Illustrated London News* for pages 20 and 29; Lincoln City Libraries and Museums Art Gallery for page 51, London Museum for page 35; Museum of Antiquities and Society of Antiquaries, Newcastle-upon-Tyne for page 78; Museum and Art Gallery, Newport, for page 65; Norwich Museum for page 74; H.G. The Duke of Wellington's Loan Collection, Reading Museum and Art Gallery for page 57; Verulamium Museum, St Albans, for pages 37 and 40–2; Trustees of the Victoria and Albert Museum for page 62; John Wacher for page 16; Graham Webster for page 63.

Introduction

When the legions of Imperial Rome invaded Britain in AD 43, their main landing was at Richborough. It is unlikely that the immense armada carrying 40,000 soldiers, camp-followers, cavalry horses, wagons, stores and equipment could have been smoothly concentrated at any one point on this hostile coast, but if the landings had been planned elsewhere for the further tactical reasons of confusing the Britons, it was a needless manoeuvre, for the landings were unopposed. Caratacus and Togodumnus, the British commanders, surprised and perhaps dismayed by the rapidity of the Roman advance westward, skirmished with their chariots while massing their forces on the Medway – probably near where Rochester now stands. Here a two-day battle was fought, and the defeated British army fled, split into two parts, the one (now leaderless, for Togodumnus had been killed in the battle) across the Thames into what is now Essex; the other, under the leadership of Caratacus, retreated to the west where his kingdom lay, in Surrey, Hampshire and the middle Thames. The victors crossed the Thames and paused for forty days to build up supplies and re-organise for the advance on Colchester, the capital of the powerful kingdom which dominated the south-eastern part of Britain. The Emperor Claudius, once the buffoon of Tiberius and Caligula, avid for military glory, now arrived to take over command. He brought with him reinforcements, including detachments of the Praetorian Guard – and elephants. The march, through Brentwood (where a battle was fought) and Chelmsford to Colchester, must have been an intimidating and unbelievable spectacle to the Britons hiding in the Essex scrubland. The orderly alignment of the troops, the horse-drawn artillery and wagon train, not less than the flashing armour and glittering standards and the huge swaying elephants, gave to those watchers a vivid foretaste of what was to be Roman Britain.

At Colchester Claudius dictated peace and received the homage of the vanquished and of those tribes who realised the hopelessness of resistance, and the advantages of being on the winning side. Even at this early stage of the invasion it was probably clear that, unlike Caesar's two raids of a hundred years before, this was to be a permanent occupation. Roman influence had already penetrated far into Britain, and even without foolish British pinpricks – there may have been raids on the Gallic coast – and disgruntled princelings who made an unwise practice of appealing to Rome, there were solid economic reasons for the exploitation of the island. Finally, there was the psychological and personal need for Claudius to have his Triumph and to establish himself, the scholar and erstwhile recluse, as a soldier and conqueror.

The campaign of Colchester lasted only sixteen days, and then Claudius, his Praetorians and his elephants left for Rome where he duly celebrated his magnificent triumph. With the capture of Colchester, the power of the Catuvellauni and their allies was broken, but there was much to be done before Roman administration and economic exploitation could function satisfactorily, so the legions and their auxiliaries fanned out to the north and west. Vespasian, later Emperor, commanded the westward drive to Silchester, Gloucester and Exeter, taking in his stride – and without very much difficulty it would seem – more than twenty hill-forts, including Maiden Castle and Hod Hill. They had not been designed to meet Roman field-artillery fire, and when the deadly ballista bolts had driven the defenders from the stockades, it was a comparatively simple matter to set ablaze the great wooden gates and storm through into the hutted enclosures. It was not all a war of conquest, for some of the tribes, the Dumnonii and the Dobunni, quickly became allies of the invaders; and further west the Britons needed Roman protection from the wild tribes of Wales: to this end a legionary fortress was founded at Gloucester in AD 48. Whilst this vigorous campaign was in progress in the south and west, columns of legionary strength and smaller formations moved north to the Humber through Cambridge and Lincoln, and into the Midlands through St Albans and Leicester to the line of the Severn and the Trent. In AD 51 Caratacus was defeated in the upper Severn Valley. He fled for protection to Queen Cartimandua of the Brigantes, who, loyal to Rome, handed him over to the conquerors. Caratacus, guilty of the crime of defending his liberty, was generously pardoned by Claudius, and ended his life in a gilded cage in Italy. Not until AD 71 was there a further thrust northward, and this the result of the defection of the Brigantes from their alliance with the Romans, to whom the Queen had fled in AD 69. The legionary fortress at York was established in AD 71 and by 79 northern Britain had been occupied. Hard fighting was necessary before the Silures in South Wales and the Ordovices in central and North Wales were conquered in AD 74–8 and the legionary fortresses at Caerleon and Chester established.

With the breakdown of the Brigantian alliance there was no longer a useful buffer state between the Roman occupied south and west and the warlike and hostile tribes to the north of Brigantia, and the Roman military mind must have envisaged the domination of what we now know as Scotland as a vast tidying-up operation. As they viewed the terrain they can have had few illusions that it would ever become commercially profitable, except perhaps as a reservoir of slaves or a recruiting ground for auxiliaries. The advance into the Lowlands began in 81 and the commander was Gnaeus Julius Agricola, whose exploits are known to us through Tacitus, his son-in-law and biographer. The years 83–84 were full of military activity by land and sea, for the fleet circumnavigated Britain, an extraordinary achievement, bearing in mind the comparatively fragile Mediterranean-type galleys and transport vessels, which were certainly unsuited to the ferocity of the northern seas.

On land the legions advanced as far north as Inverness and won a great victory over the Caledonians at Mons Graupius nearby. A legionary fortress was built at Inchtuthil on the Tay near Dunkeld. This was a critical moment for Roman Britain, with the legions poised to strike the blows which would have secured the whole of Britain for the Empire. But the Emperor Domitian decided otherwise; troops were withdrawn from Britain to reinforce the Imperial forces on the Danube, Agricola was recalled, Inchtuthil was dismantled. Under Hadrian the frontier was stabilised on the line of the Tyne and Solway Firth where the Wall positively marked the limitation of Roman rule. This was not the end of the story, for only fifteen years later, in AD 142, the Lowlands were reoccupied, and a new line of fortification was drawn across the Forth–Clyde isthmus – the Antonine Wall, which was not finally abandoned until after the conclusion of the campaigns of Severus, c.211. The Lowlands remained a sphere of Roman influence, a buffer against the wild northern tribes, until the closing years of the regime.

The long years of campaigning which achieved the conquest of Britain entailed countless marches, and the faint scars and differences in crop-markings which are visible to this day in many parts of the country attest not only to the foot-slogging valour of the legionaries, but also to the highly professional and rigidly disciplined routine which ordained that at the end of every day's march a ditch should be dug and an earth rampart raised, and that this should be topped by a stockade formed from the stakes which each man carried as part of his equipment. These marching camps, which varied in size according to the strength of the units they served, were measured precisely, and they formed concentrated and relatively secure defences against attack by the guerilla-type forces likely to be met with in Britain. The importance of the military influence on the siting of Roman towns in Britain cannot be overestimated, for in the early years of the conquest forts were constructed along lines of communication – that is to say *roads* – and at strategically important points: more than seventy such sites have been listed south of the Humber and east of the Welsh uplands. Some of them developed from temporary camps and supply depots, and towns of varying degrees of importance grew up alongside nearly all these seventy sites, and many of them are today places of considerable importance, which demonstrates very clearly the keen perceptiveness of the Roman engineers and planners. The prime objective of the Romans was, through the forming of

alliances – and where that was not possible, by conquest – to control the country and make impossible rebellion against their overall authority. It follows therefore that their thrusts (and their roads) were directed against centres of population which normally surrounded the palace of the king or chieftain. These would not have satisfied the Roman idea of a 'town' but that they were well sited for trade or topographical reasons is proved by the fact that they were confirmed in their status. Colchester, Canterbury and Silchester are instances of this continuity of occupation, but where the tribal centres were strong defensively, and so difficult to control, the population was moved to a more accessible site where any disaffection could be easily quelled. An example of this treatment was Maiden Castle, where all but a miserable remnant of the inhabitants were moved down to nearby Dorchester. What might be described as the formal planting of towns by the Romans was limited to the *coloniae* – Colchester, Gloucester and Lincoln – all formerly legionary fortresses.

The network of roads on which all these towns, trading centres, forts, posting stations and sea and river ports were strung was, without doubt, the most important and lasting result of the Roman occupation. For the first time Britain was unified and administered from the natural capital, London, which was, in fact, the focal point of the road system. The forest belts were pierced, the rivers bridged, the hills ceased to be dividing barriers, and this essential unity was never truly lost, despite Saxon kingdoms and Welsh principalities.

Britain had from the earliest times been subject to invasion, but the Roman conquest differed from all previous inroads because here for the first time was an invader from a totally alien culture, disciplined, immensely strong and with a clear objective, which was to subjugate the whole country and unite it with an economy and a culture superior to anything previously known in Britain. The Bronze and early Iron Age 'invasions' should be more properly described as 'migration' and 'infiltration', bringing with them new

methods and techniques, and, of course, warlike collisions with the older inhabitants. Successive waves of Celtic invaders appeared in Britain, and around 250 BC (that is, about one hundred years after their compatriots sacked Rome) warrior bands crossed the Channel, terrifying the British into a positive frenzy of fortification on hill-tops and around valley farm-houses. The newcomers are known to us chiefly as artists of genius (in this one respect they could more than hold their own with Greece and Rome) and their decorative bronze-work, with its swirling spirals and trumpet shapes and controlled eccentricity, is one of the high peaks of our artistic inheritance. The newcomers penetrated as far north as Yorkshire, where a tribe called the Parisi settled. In France the name is associated with Paris and they have been described as pushful and restless adventurers with a high level of civilisation. One does not usually link Leeds, Bradford and Sheffield with Paris in such an intimate way. The last wave of pre-Roman invaders were the Belgae who began to move into Britain in increased numbers when it became evident that the dynamic leadership of Julius Caesar would brook no opposition in Gaul. These refugees, for such they were, unable to cope with the legions, were yet of superior military and organising ability, and they rapidly became a dominating military aristocracy. Under Cunobelin, with his capital at Colchester, they came near to forming a national state, but on his death in c. AD 40 his kingdom was divided by his sons, and the long anticipated Roman invasion took place.

Caesar in his *Gallic War* refers rather contemptuously to a Belgic stronghold (which may have been Wheathamstead) as being set in woods and marshes, where there were 'assembled a considerable quantity of men and cattle', and he continues: 'Now the Britons call it a stronghold when they have fortified a thick-set woodland with rampart and trench, and thither it is their custom to collect, to avoid a hostile inroad.' As Caesar only penetrated into the south-eastern part of Britain, he can only have known by hearsay of the great hill-top forts of the south-west, and

perhaps not at all of the lake-villages of Somerset. The Belgic stronghold described by Caesar was probably only a temporary refuge, but there were extensive town or village sites of a more permanent kind in Britain, though the typical habitation unit was probably the farm supporting a small group of families – Little Woodbury, in Wiltshire, is a good example of this type of dwelling. It was a land of scattered small rural communities who, in times of danger, would flee to the hill-fort or stockaded fortification for protection, much as the peasants of medieval times would crowd into the castle when need arose. Cunobelin's Colchester was a grand example of a Belgic stronghold. It was defended by rectilinear earthworks enclosing an area of twelve square miles, and within this circuit an earlier curvilinear system of earthworks has been found. Cunobelin's defences were designed to counter the offensive power of the chariot, but were, of course, totally ineffective against the Roman methods of attack. It is conceivable, however, that their rectangular form may indicate a continental influence, for the circle or curve was the almost inevitable British form, and had been so from the earliest times. Buildings associated with religion, such as Stonehenge and Woodhenge, the many stone circles, domestic structures which we know from excavation, field shapes, and not least, the inimitable bronze work and jewelry – all demonstrate this instinctive preference for the curve, and it may not be too fanciful to suggest that the curve may well have influenced the shape of their villages, since it is a fact that life is but a reflection of art – or vice versa.

But if the Britons loved the curve, the Romans had a passionate predilection for the straight line and its intersection at fixed points by other straight lines at right angles to it. While it cannot be denied that the prehistoric Britons knew a great deal about geometrical construction – how else can we explain Stonehenge and Woodhenge? – it could be said that their favourite, indeed, only instrument, was a pair of compasses, but that the Romans were devoted to the T-square and the set square. Roman town-planning derived largely from Greek and Etruscan sources, and the Etruscans were undoubtedly strongly influenced by the rigid planning of the Neolithic pile villages of the Po valley. The rigidity of plan was passed on to the Romans, and we see it almost unaltered as the Roman fort, from which came the typical town-plan in Roman Britain and all the other provinces of the Empire. In addition to this close Neolithic influence, neither the Etruscans nor the Greeks could have been ignorant of the very ancient cities of the Near East with their geometrical regularity of plan; and with the powerful Greek influence in Southern Italy and the equally strong Etruscan influence in the north, it would have been surprising if the then culturally immature Romans had not adopted the ancient and admirable methods of their brilliant neighbours. All this eastern and Mediterranean influence – straight streets at right-angles forming *insulae* or islands of building, with the Greek *agora* and the Roman Forum as central focal points – was responsible for the characteristic form of the Roman towns in Britain, as indeed it was for similar foundations throughout the Roman world in Europe, Africa and Asia. To the Mediterranean man life without the town was unthinkable. The city-state had always been the norm, and, with a playing down of the ancient independent status, it was to remain until the Empire itself collapsed through old age. Furthermore, the town was used as a major instrument of the policy of Romanisation. Into it were gathered the local native nobility who then tasted the pleasures, cultural or otherwise, of civilised life, learnt the universal language, occupied various offices of local government, and met their conquerors on equal, or nearly equal, terms.

The Romans were immensely strong, completely sure of themselves and as confident in their civilising mission as were the British, and they outclassed the Britons as completely as the British did the Zulus in 1880. The conquest interfered very little with the lives of the people, who may have been relieved at the cessation of intertribal wars with their consequent slaughter and enslavement of captives.

The Romans, for their part, while enamoured of gladiatorial and wild-beast shows, did not approve of Druidical ritual human sacrifices, and the extinction of the Druids was one of the few recorded instances of Roman religious intolerance, though the political motive was probably as important as the humane aspect of this policy. Unlike the earlier folk-movements, migrations – call them what you will – the Roman conquest brought with it substantial changes: for the first time the whole country was united under one government and there was easy communication made possible by the splendid road system; perhaps as important as anything else, Britain, from being a semi-barbarous island on the edge of the known world, turned in upon itself, became (for good or ill) an integral part of a world state, and turned its face towards Europe. Very much the same thing happened at the Norman Conquest a thousand years later; then Saxon England was in disarray, ready to split into its old divisions. The Norman Conquest turned England towards Europe and the course which the Romans had set so long before was regained.

Having in mind the geometric rigidity of Roman town planning, there is a remarkable degree of variation in the towns of Roman Britain. They varied in function and constitution, and they can be divided fairly neatly into categories, but the system of provincial government needs some explanation. At the outset, Claudius behaved not only as a conqueror but as an ally, and entered into treaties with at least three powerful British rulers, King Prasutagus of the Iceni, Queen Cartimandua of the Brigantes, and King Cogidubnus of the Regni. The latter was of particular value to the invaders as it secured their western flank at an early critical stage of the campaign. All these client kingdoms had been absorbed by the end of the first century, and Roman rule, always a reality, became a legal fact. The Emperor governed the Province of Britain through a *legatus*, a man of senatorial rank, who was also the commander-in-chief. Under him were the *legati legionum*, the legionary commanders, and the *praefecti*, commanders of the auxiliary

forces. There was also a legal authority, the *legatus juridicus*, who was responsible for the administration of justice at those times when the governor was preoccupied with his military duties. And there was one other very important official, the *Procurator Augusti* in charge of finance and the collection of taxes, who was directly responsible to the Emperor, and over whom the *legatus* had no power. Julius Classicianus, who took office as *procurator* after Boudicca's rebellion (AD 60) caused the recall of the legate Suetonius Paullinus, because he viewed with alarm the draconian treatment of the defeated Iceni. That the Emperor who supported the humane policy of Classicianus was Nero gives a pretty twist to the ogre-reputation of that potentate. The tale has been spoilt by the cynical suggestion that Classicianus was more concerned with the collection of taxes than with humanity, and that he saw a disastrous fall in the Imperial revenues if the burning and slaughtering continued.

A large part of the north-east and nearly all Wales were designated as military areas, but in the remainder of the country there was a substantial degree of home-rule. Three specifically Roman towns were founded, *coloniae* of veterans at Colchester in AD 49, Lincoln in 92, at Gloucester in 97. The charter of the city settlement at York may have been granted by Severus in the first years of the third century, and this progression from civilian settlement to *colonia* was peculiar and unprecedented in Britain. These *coloniae* of veterans, who were Roman citizens, were shrewdly sited, so that in the event of a military emergency they would be able to supply a reserve of loyal trained fighting men: Gloucester on the edge of tumultuous Wales, Colchester guarding the seat of government, Lincoln and York flanking the northern military zone. The *coloniae* were small far-off echoes of the mother-city Rome, and their local government was modelled on that of the Imperial City. Magistrates were elected in pairs, theoretically by the *comitia* – the assembly of the people – but actually the magistrates chose their successors, with the sanction of the

powerful *decuriones*, one hundred in number, who formed the council or senate – the *ordo*. These councillors were men who had themselves been magistrates, or were retired centurions or men of wealth and substance with some kind of property-holding qualification, rather like those of voters in England before the Reform Bills of the nineteenth century. Evidently the administration of these *coloniae* was, in the idiom of today, something in the nature of the 'closed shop', and certainly from the second century when the *comitia* ceased to function. The magistrates, the executive officers, were in office for one year: two *duoviri iure dicundo* were concerned with the administration of justice, and two *duoviri aediles* looked after the roads, public buildings and the maintenance of order and there were probably also two *quaestores* who dealt with matters of finance. The *ordo* was kept up to its full strength by the selection, every fifth year, of eligible candidates by the two senior executive officers, who, for the occasion, adopted the title of *quinquennales*. It does not need great acuteness of perception to realise that in this organisation lay the seeds of a dangerous rigidity of structure, particularly in small communities such as these *coloniae* where the choice of candidates must have been limited: it meant the rule of a close-knit oligarchy, possible in what was fundamentally a slave economy, but offering little hope of development for the mass of the people.

Six *seviri Augustales* served as the local temple priests of the state religion, the Imperial cult, which in Britain was concentrated upon the Emperor Claudius. The central temple of the cult was built at Colchester, where its substructure still survives as the foundation of the Norman castle, and British notables were compelled to serve as priests there for annual terms and provide festivals and games in its honour. The heavy cost of these observances caused great discontent and was one of the causes of the Boudiccan revolt. After that horrific outburst the temple was rebuilt, but later it is probable that the emphasis on Claudius gave place to a more general worship of the Imperial House. In *coloniae* and *municipia* temples to the Cult would be obligatory, but elsewhere there was a merging of this cult of loyalty to the state with the worship of other gods both Roman and Celtic. In addition to the *coloniae* were the *municipia*, but the only known example in Britain is Verulamium (St Albans). It must be assumed that London received a charter at some stage. There is no clear-cut definition of Roman citizenship in *municipia*, but any such distinction vanished in AD 213 when Caracalla gave all free-born provincials that status.

Far more numerous than *coloniae* and *municipia* were the *civitates*, administrative units of local government, approximating where it was possible to the old tribal divisions. These cantonal capitals or county towns bore names which defined the territorial association; so we have Calleva Atrebatum – Calleva of the Atrebates; Venta Belgarum – Venta of the Belgae; Isca Dumnoniorum – Isca of the Dumnonii, and so on. It has been remarked that there was a distinction between the status of the chartered towns and the *civitas*, in that the former, following the Mediterranean city-state tradition, governed an area of the surrounding countryside (its *territorium*) while the *civitas* was more truly part of the tribal territory in which it was set, a point which is emphasised by the tribal attributions mentioned above. The *civitates* had their own local government, similar in essentials to that of the *coloniae*: there was an *ordo* with magistrates (who became Roman citizens on election) but no quaestors or *seviri Augustales*. That the local aristocracy, who were the *decuriones*, were primarily country gentlemen who reluctantly spent part of their time in the town, demonstrates one of those odd ineradicable continuing habits of life, and the country-loving Briton who never became the townsman is with us still.

The *vicus* and the *pagus* were also administrative units in descending order. The *vicus* with a very wide application had a governing council, but only two magistrates, and the term was applied to most settlements, including even *civitas* capitals, and also to the civil communities which grew up adjacent to forts such as Housesteads, on Hadrian's Wall,

where it occupied an area larger than the fort itself. Time-expired veterans often settled in such places and set up business, which was given added importance by the gate in the Wall nearby, through which must have flowed trade and traffic, north and south. At Corbridge (Corstopitum) the great supply-base some miles to the east of Housesteads, the *vicus* developed into a considerable town. In some instances where the fort was evacuated by its garrison, not in the face of attack, but because of a change in military policy, the *vicus* survived and flourished – this happened at Carlisle and Catterick. Large suburbs grew up adjacent to the legionary fortresses at Caerleon and Chester; and at York, a similar settlement became so important that the rank of *colonia* was granted to it. The *pagus* was, in fact, not a town but a territorial division of a *civitas*, and its modern equivalent could be 'rural district'.

The supreme formal authority in the Province – and the formality rather than the actual executive power needs to be stressed – was the *concilium provinciae* to which the *civitates* sent delegates. This national council, for such it was – the first national assembly in our history – could only give opinions and had no power to enact legislation, and its value was that through it the *legatus* could sense the feeling of the country. It was not entirely toothless, for it had the right to send complaints direct to the Emperor. The council had a voice in Rome in the person of a Senator, a *patronus* to put forward the wishes of those who lived on this island far away on the edge of the world to the august assembly (not much more powerful than the *concilium*) seated in the Curia in the shadow of the Palatine. But an important function of the *concilium* was a religious one, involving an annual celebration of the Imperial Cult at the great temple at Colchester.

Various changes in the upper structure of the administration took place in the course of the Roman occupation, but they probably had little effect upon the ordinary citizen, and one even wonders whether the Caracalla edict of 212 altered life to any appreciable extent. If his aim was to

unify the Empire after the recent struggle for supremacy, by binding all free-men together as Roman citizens, it was singularly unsuccessful, for the next hundred years was a period of acute disunity and civil war, in which Britain was not spared. In 197 Septimius Severus had divided Britain into two provinces: York became the capital of Lower Britain and London of Upper Britain. Long before this, London had supplanted Colchester as the administrative capital and the seat of government and presumably had civic honours, although at present there is no evidence of this. It was the focal point of the national road system, and whereas Colchester might be said to be on the periphery, London, easily accessible on its river, was well inside the country and ideally situated for trade. From its shanty-town foundation it thrived as a cosmopolitan gateway to Britain, as it does to this day. The Severan division of Britain into two provinces, and the later divisive arrangements had no effect on its importance – a tribute, if any were needed, to the brilliant inevitability of its siting.

But in the third century the strong light of Imperial rule began to flicker, and for a few years, under the usurpers Carausius and Allectus, Britain defied the central authority. Even in its old age, however, the Empire was still very strong, and with the defeat and death of Allectus, Diocletian reasserted control. He drastically reorganised the structure of government, which was now divided into four provinces, Britannia Prima, Britannia Secunda, Maxima Caesariensis and Flavia Caesariensis, and there may have been a fifth, Valentia, a late fourth-century location, so called in honour of the Emperor Valentinian. Britain was now designated as a *diocese*; the Governor, no longer Commander-in-Chief, was called *vicarius*. The governors of the provinces were Presidents, or *praesides*. The military commander-in-chief was now the Count of Britain, and his two subordinate commanders were the Duke of Britain, who guarded the northern frontier, and the Count of the Saxon Shore who was responsible for the defence of the south-east coast. So remote had the Emperor become that even the *vicarius* did not report to him in person but to the Praetorian Prefect of Gaul who held court at Trier. This division of command, ineffective in discouraging revolt as it proved to be, was enormously costly to operate, because of the multiplicity of courts and bureaucratic establishments which it brought into being, and in Britain, not less than in other parts of the Empire, a great deal of this cost must have fallen on the towns in the form of ever more crushing taxation. Diocletian's administration activities encompassed every aspect of life: he regulated various occupations, making them hereditary, in an effort to arrest economic and social decline, and included in these 'occupations' was the office of *decurio*. No longer sought after, this honourable and responsible association had become something to avoid because of its fearsome financial burden. In spite of the mounting problems of all kinds, there was a last glow of peace and prosperity in the Constantinian revival which followed. Then came the shattering blow of the Pictish Saxon raid of 367, and although the embattled towns were rescued by Theodosius, who drove out the barbarians and freed the captives, it must have been a serious time for Roman Britain. Yet there is evidence that even at that late date, such was the stubborn optimism of these people, there were fine new buildings being erected, in some cases in dangerously exposed areas. Many places outside the walled towns may have fallen prey to the raiders, seeking easy loot in the villas and temples, although there is very little evidence of any deliberate destruction or serious disturbance.

The towns, which had harboured the refugees from the countryside, had in the previous half century changed greatly. The large monumental structures – basilicas, temples, fora, colonnades and baths, all those public buildings, in fact, which in earlier times before the pressure of taxation had become intolerable, it had been the duty, and even, perhaps, the pleasure of the *decuriones* to give to their fellow townsmen, and to maintain – had now become ruinous and neglected, their places taken by traders' stalls and roughly

constructed dwellings. The humble folk who lived in them still prospered, but the *decuriones* now lived in their large country houses. Ironically, they too may have been among the refugees who fled to the towns, to occupy their town houses whilst the emergency lasted. It is not difficult to understand the situation which Diocletian tried to remedy. But *decuriones*, resident or non-resident, and *civitates* survived to the very end of Roman Britain, and it was to them that Honorius sent his famous rescript in 410, though hope of a restoration of imperial rule was not extinguished until 448, when the *civitates* sent a last anguished vain appeal to Aetius.

This is a difficult time to understand, but the antiquaries of earlier generations had it all worked out. Roman Britain came to an end in a blaze of destruction before the advancing Saxon hordes. Archaeology in recent years, and a closer study of the meagre and enigmatic scraps of historical evidence, has led to quite a different conclusion. Some of the great public buildings needed drastic rebuilding, but in the early fourth century some fell down, some were demolished as unsafe, others may have supplied the stone for the rebuilding of the defences under the orders of Theodosius at the end of the century. Excavations in town centres have revealed a maze of small timber structures replacing the massive masonry. When Roman imperial authority weakened and could no longer supply army units for defence, the people of Britain hired their own mercenaries, the very Saxons who had been harrying their shores; but this was a good Roman precedent. This is why Germanic burials are found in late Roman town cemeteries at places like York, Gloucester and Winchester. There may have been trouble with the rural peasants too, as there was in Gaul; here the Visigoths had been employed to suppress them. If one follows this parallel a little more closely, it seems likely that the Britons were short of cash and bullion and may have been forced to make their mercenaries substantial land grants to secure their services. This led to trouble when they demanded more, and a situation like this may be behind the famous

story of Hengist and Horsa and their dealings with Vortigern. This great British leader had succeeded in stabilising Britain by c. 430, but at a considerable price; much of Kent had to be handed over and there is a suggestion of a dynastic marriage with a Saxon princess. But the other British notables were jealous of Vortigern and there was civil strife. Throughout the troubles and turmoils of the fifth and sixth centuries life in the Roman towns continued, but it has left little archaeological trace, since the period produced very few recognisable artefacts; there were no coins and the pottery industry had collapsed with the breakdown of the capitalist economy. It is often only by the new type of buildings, the hut with the sunken floor, or very crude pottery looking like a survival from the Iron Age, that one sees the newcomers settling down with the Celtic communities. The strange myth that the Saxons came to an empty land and through superstition avoided the silent and ruined cities has long since been exploded, but will doubtless linger on in many books written by people who are out of touch with the advance of knowledge.

TOWN PLANNING

Roman towns in Britain varied greatly in size, and often in shape and plan, but they were alike in fundamentals: they were always sited on roads, the preference for the straight line and symmetry was marked, both in the structures and in their layout, and linked with this was the pronounced military character of the planning. The typical central placing of forum and basilica and the right-angled plan has already been referred to, and it is likely that this arrangement derived from the military headquarters building standing on the central cross-streets, the *via principalis* and the *via praetoria*, which led to the main gates, and which one sees in plans of all Roman forts and fortresses. In the towns, these streets were generally flanked by shops, narrow fronted buildings, packed closely together, often extending back sufficiently to allow for living accommodation and storage rooms; very often the frontages were linked to form

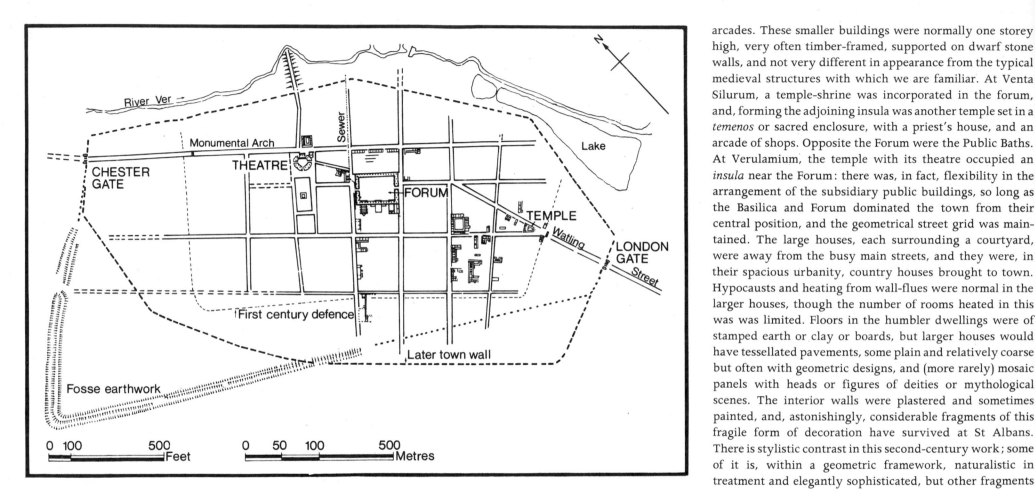

arcades. These smaller buildings were normally one storey high, very often timber-framed, supported on dwarf stone walls, and not very different in appearance from the typical medieval structures with which we are familiar. At Venta Silurum, a temple-shrine was incorporated in the forum, and, forming the adjoining insula was another temple set in a *temenos* or sacred enclosure, with a priest's house, and an arcade of shops. Opposite the Forum were the Public Baths. At Verulamium, the temple with its theatre occupied an *insula* near the Forum: there was, in fact, flexibility in the arrangement of the subsidiary public buildings, so long as the Basilica and Forum dominated the town from their central position, and the geometrical street grid was maintained. The large houses, each surrounding a courtyard, were away from the busy main streets, and they were, in their spacious urbanity, country houses brought to town. Hypocausts and heating from wall-flues were normal in the larger houses, though the number of rooms heated in this was was limited. Floors in the humbler dwellings were of stamped earth or clay or boards, but larger houses would have tessellated pavements, some plain and relatively coarse but often with geometric designs, and (more rarely) mosaic panels with heads or figures of deities or mythological scenes. The interior walls were plastered and sometimes painted, and, astonishingly, considerable fragments of this fragile form of decoration have survived at St Albans. There is stylistic contrast in this second-century work; some of it is, within a geometric framework, naturalistic in treatment and elegantly sophisticated, but other fragments are remarkable for their dense and barbaric colour and roughness of execution. One feels that this painted decoration must have been matched by heavy rich fabrics and jewelry.

AMPHITHEATRES

Many towns possessed amphitheatres, usually situated outside the town walls: they had earth banks with wooden seating for the spectators, and were larger in proportion to the towns they served than are the equivalent structures today, as though designed to serve the entire population at the same time. As they were used for civic ceremonies as well as games, this is understandable when we remember that the estimated population of Calleva is 4,000, and it is thought that 5,000 may have been the typical population limit for the larger cantonal capitals, dwindling to 3,000 for the smaller ones, and then down to a few hundreds for the less important walled towns. It has been pointed out that the population of medieval towns, in the fourteenth century, still surrounded by walls based on their Roman defences, falls into this range. The exceptions in Roman times were, of course, the few large towns, London, St Albans, Colchester and Cirencester, where populations ranging from 10,000 to 30,000 may have been normal.

THEATRES
Theatres were always within the walls: they were open to the sky, though not completely, as were the Greek theatres from which they derived, neither were they hollowed out of hillsides, but were solidly constructed of brick and stone. The stage was roofed and there was often a roofed and arcaded promenade surmounting the semi-circular auditorium.

TEMPLES
Temples were normally of the square Romano-Celtic type, with the square *cella* rising above a roofed verandah with supporting columns on dwarf walls. There were exceptions to this form, notably the great Temple of Claudius at Colchester, which was of the normal classical type, with a portico eight columns wide and four deep with side colonnades, standing on a massive podium. At St Albans there was an eccentric triangular temple, and there were a number of round and multi-angular temples and shrines in various parts of the country. The cult of Mithras, exclusive to men, and appealing particularly to the courageous

soldier, has left a few *mithraea*, some of them apparently damaged by the Christians, who regarded the cult with abhorrence because of the supposed similarity of the rituals of the two beliefs. The architectural form of the *mithraeum* closely resembled that of the basilica, with a nave and aisles and apsidal end, as it did that of the little Christian church at Silchester.

BATHS
Public bath suites, an important element in the policy of Romanisation, were sometimes included in the central building complex, as at Wroxeter, or were adjacent to it, as at Caerwent. They were very much more than bath-houses, for the Romans did not disassociate bodily wellbeing from culture and amusement and social intercourse. The great bath establishments in Rome were crowded with magnificent works of painting and sculpture, and there is no reason to think that their smaller counterparts in Britain were deficient in such attractions. Public baths were constructed on a monumental scale, as excavation has shown, and they consisted of tepid, cold and hot rooms, a sweating room, dressing room and exercise yard. It seems that the climate could not have been markedly more salubrious in Roman times than it is today, for in a number of places large roofed halls were later provided so that the contemporary keep-fit routine could be indulged in comfort.

SPAS
Bath and Buxton were two towns of exceptional character where forum and basilica must have taken second place to the great curative bath establishments. Both had been military posts, but owed their later fame and prosperity to their natural springs, which at Bath supplied a series of swimming baths with hot water from the hot water mineral springs.

THE IMPERIAL POST
The Imperial post operated on sixteen routes with its headquarters in London, and all cantonal capitals were served by couriers, gigs, coaches and wagons. *Mansiones* or posting-stations were established in the larger towns, and they were substantial complexes with their own bath-suites. A *mansio* has been identified at Silchester, near the south gate, and it occupied a larger area than any other structure, excepting the basilica and forum. Along the roads there were changing stations where fresh horses could be obtained. All this elaborate organisation was provided by the *civitates*, and with the upkeep of the roads for which they were also responsible, must have been a considerable charge on the local exchequers.

BASILICA AND FORUM
Temples, baths, town-houses, arcaded shopping streets, posting-stations, theatres and amphitheatres and the enclosing fortifications were dominated by the great central monumental block of basilica and forum. We are very familiar with the basilican form because it was the prototype of the earliest Christian churches – a central nave, side aisles with arcades and with the apsidal ends slightly raised above the floor level of the nave. Ranged in a half-circle against the end wall were the seats of the judges and assessors, with the raised seat of the *praetor* in the centre. On the chord of the half-circle was an altar where sacrifices were offered before the commencement of the day's business, for the basilica was the judicial and administrative centre of the town, and meeting place of merchants, rather like the London Guildhall of 200 years ago. On one of its long sides was a range of offices, and on the opposite side were the main doors giving on to the Forum. This was the social centre, and here the typical Roman tendency to enclose space with walls and colonnades led to that busy concentration of people and interest and activity which was characteristic of them and all their works. Behind the arcades of columns on three sides of the square were open-fronted shops and paved pro-

menades sheltered from the elements, and on the side fronting the street there would be a wide arched monumental entrance. On market days booths and stalls would be erected in the square, and it does not need much imagination to envisage a scene of animation and noisy activity, with a rather grand and formal background, carrying with it a feeling of security to the colourful crowds. 'Colourful' needs to be stressed because we are too apt to think of Roman life, whether in Britain, where it was a synthesis of Roman and Celtic cultures, or in Italy itself, as having a blanched, somewhat frigid appearance, and this is partly due to our having been conditioned by the innumerable so-called historical paintings, in which the artists have accepted the whiteness of sculptural remains as indicative of their original hue. Nothing, of course, could be less true of ancient life and art, any more than it is of medieval architecture and sculpture: only today has colour lost its vital role in life, despite the gallant efforts of the young.

DRAINAGE

The Romans have a great reputation for their drainage and water supply systems, though they were in no way the originators of what has been a natural preoccupation of town builders from the most ancient times; one need only cite the highly sophisticated drainage systems discovered at Knossos, dating from about 1400 BC, to demonstrate this historical fact. Excavation has disclosed no evidence for general sewerage systems in the majority of the cantonal capitals, though individual buildings and the public baths had their own sewers, sometimes, as at Wroxeter, flushed by surplus water from roadside leets. At Venta Silurum a drainage channel ran along the side of the main street, and may have served houses and the public baths: it is thought that it was covered by stone flags. An exceptionally complete drainage system has been discovered at Lindum; stone-built sewers complete with man-holes and feeders from private houses served all the main streets. At Colchester and St Albans large-scale sewers have also been found, but it is interesting to note that a highly developed chequerboard street plan, and important public and private buildings did not inevitably or even generally mean that a comprehensive drainage system was necessarily a concomitant. When one studies inscribed tombstones of the Roman period it becomes clear that the life-span was very short, as short, indeed, as in medieval times, notorious as non-bathing, plague-ridden and thoroughly unhygienic centuries, and one wonders whether, perhaps the high reputation of the Romans for what may be called 'hygienic superiority' has been overstressed.

WATER SUPPLY

The towns were adequately supplied with water, sometimes through open leets or water-wheels, pumps or even aqueducts, and, of course, wells were an important source of supply. In London, for instance, the area to the west of Walbrook was dotted with timber-lined wells, whose contents must have been dangerously tainted, since it is probable that the Walbrook itself could have been little better than an open drain. Silchester, Caerwent and St Albans were probably served by aqueducts, as were other towns in Roman Britain, though it is difficult to visualise them, particularly in areas where building stone was in short supply, where they may well have been of timber construction. Distribution tanks inside the town received the water from the aqueduct, and from them the water was piped to where it was needed: traces of these wooden pipes joined together by iron collars have been found. At Lincoln water was pumped uphill from a spring more than a mile from the town into a large tank – and the pipes were sealed in waterproof concrete to withstand pressure!

TOWN WALLS

Lastly, but not least in importance, is the problem of the massive fortifications which surrounded towns both great and small – the problem being one of dating and the intricacies of Imperial policy, conditioned and interrupted by rebellions and the secession of mutinous governors. The primary objective of the Roman invaders was to bring the native population under control (in other words, to tame them) and, therefore, where there were defiant fortified hill-forts they were stormed, and the inhabitants transferred to a more accessible and easily dominated site. In the early years of the conquest following the subjugation of the Britons and the general pacification which followed, the last thing the Romans wanted was for the new towns and existing cantonal capitals or any other centres to be fortified. The Roman policy, understandably, was to leave the Britons defenceless. Even Colchester the provincial capital, London bursting at the seams with valuable imports and the key to the strategic control of Britain, and St Albans, a very early centre of Romanisation, were without effective defences. For they had defences which were more in the nature of lines of demarcation than protection against assault, as was found to their cost when Boudicca utterly destroyed them in AD 60, nearly twenty years after the conquest. If it was thought desirable to leave these large Romanised towns without defences, it is obvious that sanction for general fortification would not be given – for this was a matter of Imperial policy, and not of local choice. Only one cantonal capital had first-century earthworks, and that was Silchester, where they were, perhaps, allowed as a recognition of loyalty at the time of the rebellion; and the *coloniae* because of their unique link with Rome, would probably have received the privilege of fortification at an early date. But it was not until the end of the second century that widespread building of earthwork town defences took place, and it looks as if the circuits of these defences were laid out by military engineers and that there was no time for masonry. The stone parts to the banks were added later but not in all cases. This gave the towns, large and small, their final form which survived in many cases until they burst their ancient bonds in modern times. These new walls supported on their inner sides flat-topped earthbanks. Outside, continuous ditches were dug, often in duplicate or triplicate. This final demarcation meant the curtailment of some towns, and certainly the limitation of growth in others. At Silchester, for instance, the over-ambitious chequerboard street plan can still be traced outside the line of fortification. It can be said that Albinus, fearing a Pictish inroad while his forces were fighting on the continent, might rapidly throw up these earth banks to give some sort of security to the Britons. On the other hand the stone walls show no evidence of haste, but are of splendid construction throughout. What one is entitled to wonder at is the size of the labour force involved, the skilled masons, surveyors, stone-cutters – that is the marvellous aspect of this problem.

The Roman administration must have thought this comprehensive fortification of British towns long overdue, for, highly desirable as it was for the large towns, it was the smaller towns, the local taxation centres, the posting-stations and road junctions which needed protection from petty revolts and brigandage. All this work was enormously costly to the *civitates*, and the *decuriones* must have groaned aloud. These circumvallations were examples of passive defence, and the townsfolk could close their gates and sleep secure. There was no need to fight to preserve themselves from ill-disposed persons, and the slightest of home-guards could man the walls until help came from the nearest army post. To the north, of course, were the barbarian Picts, and the Welsh were always liable to be troublesome, but the army could deal with these and the military zones were buffers that existed for the specific purpose of protecting the richer parts of the province. But, unfortunately, times were changing, and no sooner had this comfortable security become established, when, in the second half of the fourth century barbarian pressure on the frontiers, both sea and land, became yearly more menacing, and culminated in the devastating concerted raid by Picts and Saxons in 367, already referred to. Count Theodosius expelled the invaders and carried out a great reconstruction throughout the province, and not the least of his achievements were the changes he brought to the whole conception of town

defence. The towns had survived the storm, but perhaps only because the influx of sturdy refugees from the countryside had made possible a manning in strength of their long walls, and passive defence in the new conditions had to be superseded by a system which, while economical in manpower, could by aggressive action fight off the now powerful barbarian menace, for there can have been no illusions regarding the bleak future. The solution of this problem was simple enough – the addition of artillery platforms, or bastions, projecting from the wall face, from which *ballistae* on swivel mountings could not only direct covering fire along the wall face, but subject an attacking force to heavy converging bombardment. This was following the military precedent of the late third-century Saxon Shore Forts where round-fronted bastions were an integral part of the design. The old town-ditches, set close to the walls and invariably V-shaped, were re-cut, up to 100 feet wide and shallow, with flat bottoms and affording no cover to the attackers, but forming veritable death traps. The *ballistae* (which were huge cross-bows) had an effective range of 600 feet and were probably served by regular soldiers. Thus, an ominous sign, the towns in these later years of Roman Britain became fortresses.

Evidently there was still much to defend, and the now well-fortified towns may have lived on as dwindling communities in their crumbling ruins until they were taken over by the powerful Saxon mercenaries who had been established in the towns in the fourth century to protect them against invaders.

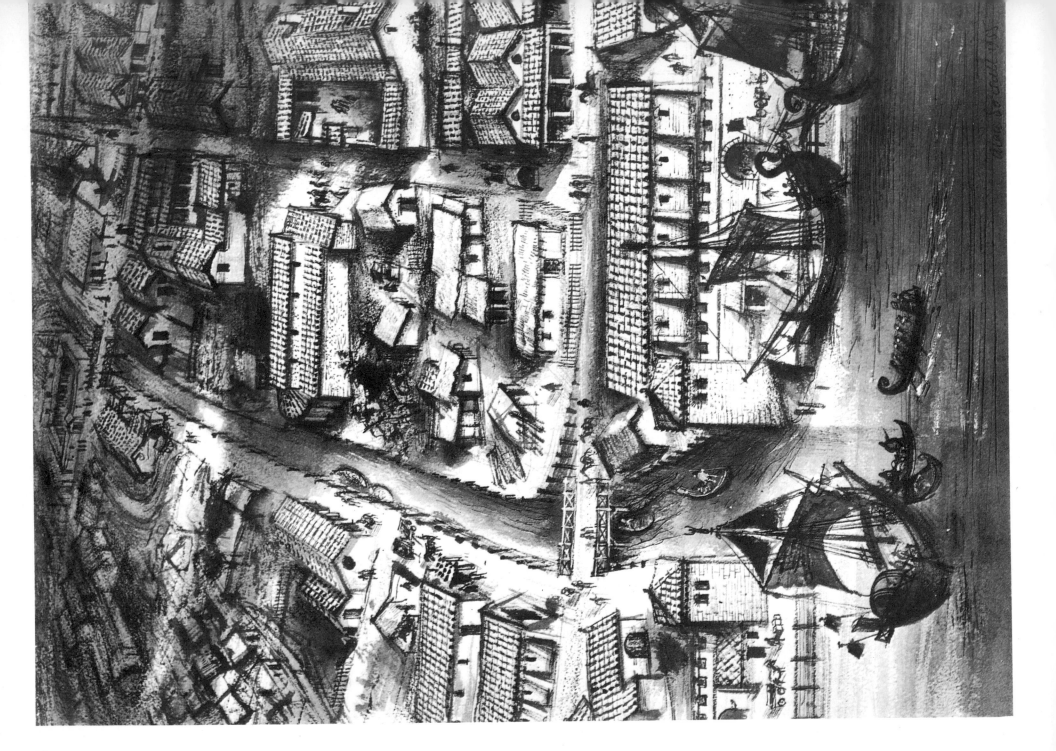

London (Londinium)

Londinium is the Latinised form of the Celtic Londinos, a hypothetical personal name formed from *londo*, meaning 'fierce'; but archaeological opinion is against the assumption of a Celtic foundation, since the pre-Roman remains along the river banks are, so far, meagre and scattered. The tidal flood of the Thames (which today reaches Teddington) in Roman times only reached the site of the city; the river was fordable at this point and furthermore the banks were of hard gravel, well suited for bridging. The Thames, penetrating deeply into Britain, was ideally suited for carrying trade. The site of Londinium was open to the south and protected on the north by rising land covered with a thick oak forest. Although claims have been made that Caesar crossed the Thames at Brentford or Walton, it is more probable that he used the ford at London, as did the army of Claudius in AD 43. Two low hillocks rising to a mere thirty feet above river level were the eastern and western limits of the city. Leadenhall Market covers the eastern hill, as did the Forum in Roman times, and St Paul's Cathedral surmounts the western hill. There were two smaller hillocks to the east where the Tower of London and the Mint now stand, the latter outside the city walls. The site was bisected north and south by the Walbrook flowing into the river: Londinium was bounded on the west by the Fleet river. To the north the tributaries of the Walbrook created a marshy area which was to be greatly enlarged in medieval times. Londinium was never a fortress, though it was a temporarily fortified supply base in Claudian times and transit base from the time of Trajan. In its early years it was, and indeed ever remains, the city of the bridge, that all-important link between south and north and the unifying bonding chain of the Province. From the earliest years of the conquest Londinium was a busy cosmopolitan port – a shanty town of ancient times. In those early years it could have had little dignity of architecture or planning, only the teeming energetic get-rich-quick character of traders, from all parts of the Empire, with troops passing through, or returning from campaigns up country. However, seventeen years after the conquest, the thriving city was utterly destroyed by Boudicca's Iceni and Trinovantes, and a layer of red ash and fragments of pottery, Claudian coins fused by the great heat and wall plaster, have been found in the area of Gracechurch Street and Walbrook. As the British host drew near, the citizens had the choice of abandoning all their possessions and fleeing to Gaul, or following the Roman forces to their point of concentration in the west, or remaining in the city. Those who did this were slaughtered, and London was ringed with the crucified victims of Boudicca's vengeance. When London was reoccupied – for the inevitable Roman counter-blow was rapid and ruthless – it was rebuilt in a larger and more splendid form than the Claudian city: where timber and wattle had been normal, now stone took their place.

THE STREETS

Traces of a typical Roman grid-pattern of streets have been found in London, and the establishment of this pattern has been greatly helped by the natural assumption that streets led to the gates whose positions were positively established; so an approximately north by south, and east by west grid has been pieced together. But one's instinctive thought in looking back to the very earliest years of the Roman occupation is that, when the legions marching up from the south came over the bridge, they debouched north-west and north-east as well as marching more directly to the north. In other words, there must surely have been an earlier diagonal pattern of roads coming from the bridge, and the typical Roman grid was superimposed on it. But there is very little surviving evidence of this rational plan except for traces of a gravel road on timber foundations running approximately north-west, which does, indeed, exactly conform to the bridge-diagonal pattern. In its presumed direction, based on the evidence of building fragments found at the junction of Bread Lane and Watling Street, it tends to bend towards Ludgate rather than Newgate. To the north-east of the bridge, however, nothing has been discovered which encourages the idea of an Aldgate-Bridge diagonal, so all that can be said is that, whilst some small evidence exists for this rational diagonal plan, there is evidence also for its submergence by the grid-plan. For the latter we have conclusive evidence. From the east end of the Forum, running north to Bishopsgate and Ermine Street, a well-marked length of gravel metalling 25 feet wide has been found made up to no less than eight feet in thickness, which would seem to indicate continual resurfacing over a very long period of time. To the west of the Basilica and Forum, indications of another north-south road have been noted, whilst to the south of the Forum, running east and west, and continuing along the line of Bucklersbury, fragments of a well-defined street pointing to Newgate have been unearthed. A portion of this street was found by Sir Christopher Wren when he was digging the foundations for the new church of St Mary-le-Bow after the great fire of 1666. He reported 'a Roman Causeway of rough stone, close and well rammed with Roman Brick and Rubbish at the Bottom, for a Foundation, and all firmly cemented'. So sure was Wren of the stability of this ancient fragment that he laid the foundation of his delicate fantasy of a tower directly upon it. From St Martin le Grand along Newgate Street there are traces of gravel road metalling leading directly to the gate and the road to Silchester and the west. Cannon Street exactly overlies an east-west element in the grid. Walbrook was probably bridged at two points, though no traces of these, presumably timber, structures, have survived. The streets varied in width from 18 to 35 feet. They were made with local gravel mixed with concrete which resulted in an almost rock-like hardness. They were cambered, with gullies along the sides, and they were probably flanked by paved sidewalks, which in some cases may well have been protected by colonnades. The streets were linked by a network of alleys very similar in character to those of medieval London, some of which still survive.

THE BASILICA AND FORUM

The Basilica was the focal point of Roman London, physically as well as administratively, since it was sited so that the

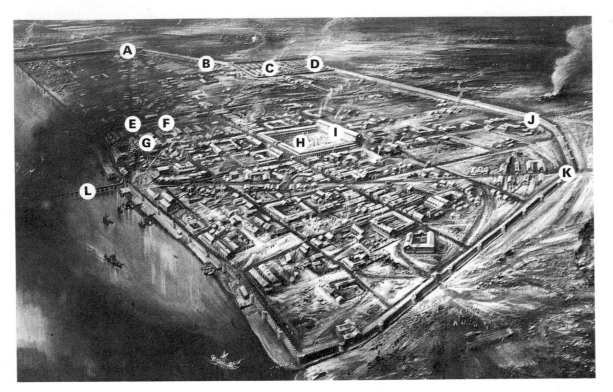

A	Newgate	G	Governor's Palace
B	Aldersgate	H	Forum
C	Fort	I	Basilica
D	Cripplegate	J	Bishopsgate
E	Walbrook	K	Aldgate
F	Mithraeum	L	London Bridge

Roman London in about A.D. 400. The snow-bound city, with burning houses ▶
beyond the walls, fired by Saxon raiders

A typical street scene in
Roman London

traveller from the south, on crossing the bridge, would have seen its great bulk immediately before and above him at the top of the hill which we now call Cornhill, where Leadenhall Market now stands. The Basilica was 500 feet long, about the same length as St Paul's Cathedral. It was aligned east and west, parallel to the river, and must have towered above the surrounding buildings as did St Paul's before the construction of the hideously dreary office blocks which now brutally disfigure the city.

The Basilica had a total width of 150 feet, including a range of what were probably administrative offices on its north side. It was aisled. The excavated walls, however, present some confusing features: there is an unaccountable double wall extending nearly half way along the south side, and a difference in date has been detected between the various fragments which have been found in this area. It is now thought that the south aisle was open to the Forum and took the form of an open arcade. This would have meant that the Basilica, or a large portion of it, would have been in effect an extension of the Forum as a meeting place and promenade. One must suppose, however, that some portion of the Basilica would have been completely walled – it is difficult to visualise legal and administrative processes functioning in a brisk westerly gale. Archaeological opinion has now generally agreed that the Basilica was built about AD 80–90, and was extended westwards to its full length of 500 feet in the early second century. Evidence in the form of a thick layer of ash has been found on the site of the Basilica, which suggests that the devastating fire which occurred in the early second century may have destroyed the earlier building and so have been the reason or excuse for the extension westwards. The Basilica summed up in one great structure all the administrative and legal functions of the state, unlike our present usage which houses law courts and government under separate roofs. In addition the Basilica was the meeting place of the merchants, rather like the Guildhall of 200 years ago. The architectural form of the Basilica, with its aisles separated from the central space, or nave, by rows of columns, and with its apsidal ends, was, of course, the prototype of the early Christian churches of the west.

The Basilica occupied the north side of the great open space of the Forum. They cannot be disassociated, the one from the other, and the Forum might be described as the *atrium* or forecourt to the Basilica. Rows of shops and offices were on the south-west and east sides of the Forum, linked and protected by a colonnaded walk. Centrally in the south side there would have been a monumental entrance and in the middle of the square probably a rostrum or an altar flanked by columns crowned by gilded statues. This architectural formality was qualified, no doubt, by the temporary stalls and booths set up on market days and festivals. Archaeological evidence shows that the Forum in its final development dates from Hadrianic times, and substantial traces of its south wall and arcade have been found along the line of Lombard Street where it meets Gracechurch Street. That the building of this Hadrianic Forum made necessary the demolition of earlier buildings of various dates has been demonstrated by the discovery of their fragmentary remains.

THE GOVERNOR'S PALACE

Cannon Street Station has submerged if not obliterated the western half of a late first-century complex of buildings which have been called, fancifully, but not without some rationality, the 'Governor's Palace'. The recently excavated fragments are bounded on the east by Suffolk Lane, on the south by Upper Thames Street, and on the north by Cannon Street. In a central position on the site are the extremely massive remains of a hall measuring 50 by 95 feet, with the longer axis north and south. To the east (and, it is presumed, to the west also) is a fragmentary apsidal structure connected with the central hall by massive walls. To the north and south there were large courtyards enclosed by a quadrilateral of colonnaded buildings comprising a great number of small rooms with indications of staircases which suggest an upper storey. In the south courtyard a great walled pool with its floor six feet below the courtyard level has been identified, with the base of what may well have been a fountain in a rounded projection on its north side – or rather *two* foundations, for bearing in mind the Roman passion for symmetry in architectural form, one may assume that beneath Cannon Street Station lies, or lay, the other complementary half of this Governor's Palace complex. Excavators of the site, whether they have been sewer diggers, railway engineers or archaeologists, have commented on the enormously massive construction of the walls: one discovered in 1840 was 20 to 26 feet in width, and when the railway station was being built in 1868 'an immense external wall' 200 feet long, 10 feet high and 12 feet thick running east and west was found, together with cross walls and the remains of apartments with tessellated pavements and wall paintings. The land sloped steeply towards the river in this area, and seems to have been terraced in Roman times, but the courtyards were level, and the south courtyard was built up as a platform of 'flint and ragstone rubble concrete 6–7 feet thick' (Merrifield). Tiles stamped PP.BR.LON. (Procurator or Portoria Provinciae Britanniae, Londinium) were found and these suggest that they were used in a Government building. The Emperor Hadrian may have stayed in this palace during his visit to Britain in AD 122.

The fort, probably built during the Principate of Trajan AD 98–117, was only discovered as the result of German bombing 1940–1944, which laid bare the foundations of the Cripplegate area, when Professor Grimes showed that the curious kinks in the city wall were to link up the walled fort already there. It was then seen that the fort measured 280 yards from north to south and 238 from east to west, with its *via praetoria* perpetuated by Wood Street and *via principalis* by Silver Street and Addle Street. Cripplegate is in the exact position of the ancient North Gate. The fort, away from the river and the bridge, is oddly sited, but in those expansive Trajanic days it is probable that defences were a minor

consideration. It may have been a transit-supply base or fort for the governor's guard and staff, most of whom were on secondment from the army.

THE WALBROOK MITHRAEUM

Londinium was the largest town in Roman Britain with a walled area of 330 acres equalled by only four other Roman towns north of the Alps, but very little of it remains, precisely because its perfect siting meant that all through the ages there has been continual rebuilding and consequently destruction of earlier structures. The Walbrook Mithraeum, discovered by Professor Grimes in 1952, was the most sensational find of the century, capturing the public imagination and drawing enormous crowds to see it. The archaeologists have, however, very mixed feelings since the pressure of public interest did interfere with building progress, and, thereafter, many contractors ordered their workmen to keep quiet about any similar finds. Apart from the remarkable building the excavation gave a view of the Walbrook Valley with its network of streams. It was a wet and, in places, marshy area with alder thickets – a very odd state of affairs in the middle of the provincial capital. The Mithraeum had been built on the edge of the Walbrook at the end of the second century and was a long rectangular building of basilican plan, almost 60 feet long and 26 feet wide, with an apse at the west end, supported by three massive buttresses. There was a vestibule at the east end projecting beyond the width of the main buildings, but this was not possible to excavate. The building underwent a long period of alterations, during which the floor was successively raised over three feet. But it remained quite unlike the *mithraea* one finds in the frontier areas, which are small underground structures simulating the celestial vault and the rock 'from which the god was born'. The Walbrook was not the place of the sworn brotherhood of soldiers, but more suited the easy familiarity of shopkeepers and merchants who were not seeking aid in battle conditions, but mutual trust in commerce. The use of the building ceased in the middle of the fourth century, when its worshippers were probably under serious attack from the Christians.

Some of the precious sculptures and implements of ritual were carefully buried under the floor. Among these sculptures was the head of the god with its Phrygian cap, a superb marble of Jupiter Serapis, the merchant's god. There were other deities clearly indicating the cosmopolitan character of the worshippers. But perhaps the most exciting find was a small silver gilt canister with a strainer, decorated with hunting scenes in relief. This object used in temple ritual is unique: it was found as a crushed and mangled meaningless piece of corroded metal, and as such was sent to the conservation laboratory in the British Museum and the excavators forgot all about it, until one day, many months later, it was produced beautifully cleaned and restored to its original shape. (There is an excellent chapter on the discovery of this building by Professor Grimes in his book *The Excavation of Roman and Medieval London*, 1968.) For the rest there is a suite of baths in Cheapside, part of another in Lower Thames Street which has been preserved, a growing number of stone and timber buildings, and the inevitable wells, all showing extensive and fairly dense occupation, while along the main roads outside the defences there are large cemeteries.

THE DEFENCES

The Roman linear defences of London are exactly defined by the later medieval city, except for a diversion between Ludgate and the river, where they were demolished by the Black Friars, with the permission of King Edward I, to give space for the enlargement of the precinct of their priory. The Roman walls were pierced by Ludgate, Newgate, Aldersgate, the north gate of the fort – which we know as Cripplegate – then Aldermanbury Postern, which in all probability was of Roman origin. Moorgate was enlarged from a medieval postern into a gateway in 1415, and was not Roman in foundation. Bishopsgate and Aldgate were both Roman, and so, it is thought, was the Tower Postern, between Aldgate and the river. All the gateways noted above, with the exception of the two posterns, served Roman roads or, as in the case of Aldersgate, earlier roads which continued in use in Roman times.

We have no positive evidence of the date of the construction of the defences but, as we have seen, the governership of Clodius Albinus, the rival of Severus, from 192 to 197, has been suggested as the most likely date for logistic reasons – the expectation of attack by Severus – and the evidence of coins and pottery found in the internal earthbank, which is thought to have been of the same period as the wall it supported. The external projecting bastions, a reversion to a much earlier type of urban fortification, were added in the late fourth century. These bastions, some solid, on the east, others hollow, were on the east and west flanks of the defences, with only two bastions, with an interval of 800 yards between them, on the north. Solid bastions were an important feature of late Roman defensive works, and they were so constructed as to be suitable as mountings for heavy *ballistae* which could fire along the intervening lengths of wall and so take attackers in the flank. They were interdependent, and made possible successful defence with very small forces. The western group of bastions were hollow in construction, and these, it is now thought, may be of post-Roman date. No archaeological explanation has so far been made to account for the limitation of bastions on the northern wall, other than the 'chance of non-discovery'.

The Roman wall was constructed of Kentish ragstone with a plinth of Kentish sandstone. Its core was of ragstone in its rough state set in extremely hard white mortar 'which was perhaps run into the core in a fluid state as the interstices are not completely filled' (Wheeler). This solid mass was faced externally and internally with squared and coursed ragstone blocks with an approximate measurement of nine by five inches. At three-foot vertical intervals there were triple bonding courses of Roman bricks and these were carried through the wall. Where the bonding courses occurred, the wall was reduced in thickness internally by

Professor and Mrs Grimes examining the newly unearthed
Temple of Mithras in London

about three inches. Thus an effect of entasis was produced which was pleasing aesthetically, although of little structural significance. Whatever were the conditions of emergency which dictated the building of the wall, they were evidently not allowed to interfere with such subtleties.

The wall stands upon a foundation of flints and puddled clay in a trench three to four feet deep cut in the natural ground. There is no absolute evidence as to the height of the wall – its highest remaining fragment recorded was about 16 feet above the plinth – but it is reasonable to suppose that to the tops of the battlements which protected the wall walk it reached a height of not less than 20 feet, whilst the thickness varied from seven to nine feet. It may be here mentioned that the height of Hadrian's Wall has been estimated as 21 feet six inches, with a mean thickness of nine feet – the latter measurement also applies to the city wall of Verulamium, and it seems likely that the dimensions of defensive walls were standardised. The usual Roman method of wall construction was to assign lengths of wall to separate gangs of workmen, and Wheeler has pointed out that this procedure is indicated in the London Wall by the faulty joining up of the bonding courses at various points. The remains of the towered gateways are scanty: only at Newgate and Aldersgate are there surviving foundations of any importance, and these demonstrate that the two gates were of a totally different form from each other. In a separate category are the remains of the west gate of the fort, and these will be referred to later.

At Bishopsgate what may have been the wall of a gatehouse projecting about 20 feet inside the wall has been found. The Newgate remains are of a simple rectangular structure measuring 95 by 32 feet with double gate passages. Like Aldersgate, Newgate was set awkwardly at an angle to the wall so that, whilst its northern end projected seven feet beyond it, its southern end stood fully 14 feet. It would have been normal for the ditch to have been spanned by a timber bridge wide enough to allow unimpeded access to the two gate passages – one for inward

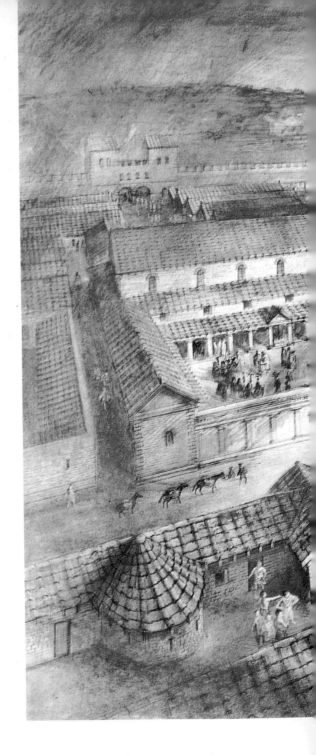

and the other for outward traffic. Aldersgate bore some resemblance to the east and west gates of Verulamium. Its sharply projecting rounded gate towers indicate a later date than Newgate's simple rectangle. Aldersgate was related to the wall even more awkwardly than Newgate and it was clearly inserted into the defences when they were already in existence. The Roman ditch system normally had two periods, two or three V-shaped ditches superseded by a much wider single ditch when the bastions were added. The earlier ditches varied in width from 10 to 16 feet, the later ditch was further widened and altered in the Middle Ages and this makes it difficult to reconstruct the original profile.

There are, at various points along the river frontage, substantial remains of Roman walls, and it has been observed that because of the instability of the river bank special constructional methods were used, including massive timber reinforcements designed to resist the tendency of the heavy structure to slide or topple into the soft mud of the river bank. Wheeler, quoting *Archaeologia*, LXIII, records the structure of this supposed river wall in some detail: 'Large roughly squared timbers, 12 feet long and about 8 inches square, were first laid on the top of the ballast across the thickness of the wall, these being in position by pointed piles driven in at intervals . . . on these timbers were laid large irregular sandstones and ragstones bedded in clay and flints . . . above which was a bond of two rows of yellow tiles . . . chalk and other stone formed the core, the whole being cemented with red mortar.'

Further to the west of the structure described above, two fragments of massive wall were examined by Roach Smith in 1839–41. They were 360 yards apart, and in exact alignment along the river frontage. In 1961, a series of great walls was discovered adjacent to one of these fragments – in the Lambeth Hill area – and it is now believed that these walls together with the Roach Smith fragment formed part of some huge platform or quay. A right-angled turn to the north (which had, in fact, been noted by Roach Smith) is thought to be proof that no continuous riverside defensive

wall existed in Roman times. However, an early medieval chronicler, the twelfth-century Fitzstephen, wrote confidently that 'on the south side also the Citie was walled and towred, but the fish full river of Thames with his ebbing and flowing hath long since subverted them', and though it cannot be proved that Fitzstephen referred to Roman walls and towers the strong probability remains. This vexed question was solved in 1975 when a long length with many raised sculptured stones was exposed in the process of development. It has been pointed out that the fragmentary Roman city land-wall points directly towards the Lanthorn Tower (which was in medieval times the corner tower of the Tower of London's inner curtain), and it has been suggested that the Wakefield, Bell and Middle Towers extending westward at the appropriate intervals are perhaps founded upon Roman bastions, though here again current archaeological opinion is opposed to the idea. This great defensive system can be described as the abiding Roman contribution to the shape of London.

Surprisingly little is known of the history of Roman London. Tacitus, Ammianus Marcellinus the historian and Ptolemy the geographer mention Londinium in their own days (the first-second century A D). Eumenius the private secretary of Constantius Chlorus lets in a pinpoint of light to illumine Londinium desperately beset in the late third century, after the collapse of the short-lived British Empire. The city is mentioned in the Antonine Itinerary in the early third century as the focal point of the British road system. A Bishop of London attended the Council of Arles in A D 314, and the *Notitia Dignitatum* of 300–428 (wide dating since it is a compilation) mentions the 'officer in charge of the Treasury at Augusta (London)', an indication of the importance of the city at that later date, and there are two Byzantine references to 'Lindonion' and 'Londinium Augusti'. Nothing further is recorded until the medieval chroniclers begin their fabulous legends, some of which may be far off distorted echoes of real historical happenings. We know

nothing of the decay of the great structures in the city, but we do know that the fortifications were energetically maintained, and this means that there was much left to defend, and that there was the will to do so. It is unlikely that London was ever abandoned – Saxon houses in the walled city have been found in excavations – but the situation may in its smaller way have resembled the later years of Constantinople when, surrounded by Turkish conquests, and with a Turkish section in the city, it still maintained a precarious life of its own. Constantinople was finally conquered, but Roman Celtic London may have been saved from such a dramatic end by the presence of a strong Saxon community later converted to Christianity, and the bishopric was revived in 604 by St Augustine.

The creation of the Department of Urban Archaeology in the Guildhall Museum has led to a continuing succession of excavations on sites under threat of development and already important results are being made and recorded in regular reports issued by the Museum. Much has been learnt from a series of riverside quays of the Roman period, especially on the problems of the changes in the river level and line of the bank.

Newgate, looking north-east towards the Cripplegate Fort

St Albans (Verulamium)

Verulamium, today St Albans, is one of those towns, of which Colchester and Silchester are important instances, with pre-Roman origins. The site of Roman Silchester coincided almost exactly with that of its Belgic predecessor, but at Colchester and St Albans the new Roman settlements had grown up beside the earlier towns, and had, in effect, destroyed them by absorbing their population and administrative functions. At Verulamium the Belgic town lay to the north and north-east of the Roman site on a plateau rising from the valley of the River Ver, and known today as Prae Wood. Time has not been able to erase the traces of extensive banks and ditches which survive there overgrown by woodland: the earlier phase of these Belgic earthworks has been dated at the end of the first ventury BC. It had long been thought (Camden, the Elizabethan archaeologist, was responsible in the first instance for the attribution) that the Prae Wood earthworks were fragments of the oppidum of Cassivelaunus which was taken by Julius Caesar in 54 BC. But Wheathamstead, five miles to the north-east, has now been more confidently identified as the fortress-town mentioned in the *Gallic War*. It is possible that the later earthworks at Prae Wood are of the period of the Claudian invasion of 43 AD, when a frantic attempt seems to have been made to give them an essentially military form.

Some time after Caesar's more or less abortive invasions of 55 and 54 BC, Wheathamstead gave place to Verulamion, which became the Catuvellaunian capital, only to be superseded in its turn by Camulodunum, which was more advantageously placed as a sea port to deal with the increasing trade with the Roman world. Today we should describe this Roman trade penetration as a 'softening-up process', for not only Roman goods but Roman ideas came into Britain in this way, and were important steps towards the inevitable military take-over. Meanwhile, the royal house of Cunobelinus ruled an expanding kingdom in splendour. Verulamium appears to have remained a flourishing place, though of less political eminence than before. The defences, hastily contrived, could not have caused the Romans very much trouble, and probably the town submitted soon after the triumphal entry of Claudius into Camulodunum.

The road makers dictated the siting of Roman towns in Britain, as elsewhere, and when the legions pushed north and west from their base-camp at Colchester, Watling Street was driven up and along the valley of the Ver below the Belgic town. Belgic Verulamion had come into being primarily to command the ford, which still exists and is known as St Michael's ford, and it was a certainty that the Romans, with their keen eye for locality, would recognise the importance of the river crossing; in fact, Roman Verulamium became the junction of roads, south to Londinium, north to the Midlands and the whole of the northern part of the Province, east to Welwyn, Braintree and Colchester, west to Silchester and thence to the south-west and to Wales. Today we are apt to overlook the significance of river crossings and similar natural direction pointers, but in ancient – and not so ancient – times they were vital. Watling Street, for such is the extremely inappropriate name that has from time immemorial been applied to this major Roman road, skirted, at a distance of half a mile, the long banks and ditches of the Belgic town to the west, and closely followed the course of the Ver on the east. Across the river the land rises, but the river valley must have been marshland. Camden writes of Verulamium in his day as being 'fortified by woods and marshes', and these river marshes were the only natural defences possessed by the Roman town, which was sited on the long slope westward toward Prae Wood.

In the years following the conquest, when it seemed that south-eastern Britain had been pacified, and the legions were far away, thrusting into Wales and fighting in the north, the Roman town came into being. Its nucleus seems to have been a fortified post – it would have been remarkable if the ford had been left unguarded even in those days of peace – and traces of a bank revetted with timbers and a wooden watch-tower have been found, together with material related to the reigns of Claudius and Nero. The existence of this post, defended by earthworks, can well explain the odd oblique angle taken by Watling Street to avoid it, though it is surprising that a small fortification, clearly only of a temporary nature, should have been allowed to deform – permanently – the great main road from London to the north. In those early days the conjunction of road and fort, with the promise of trading of all kinds, must have been an irresistible attraction to the remainder of the population of the old town to move down into the valley: that they did so is proved by the large quantities of Belgic pottery and other objects including coin moulds have come to light, and we can envisage ribbon development along the road: shops, houses and warehouses, an inn, a temple perhaps, then administrative buildings of some kind. Growth must have been extremely rapid, for by AD 60 Verulamium had become a *municipium*, 'the highest rank which Rome could award to a native foundation' according to Tacitus. Verulamium remains the only certain *municipium* in Britain. It is conceivable that this grant of municipal status by Claudius was a calculated Imperial gesture of confidence in the Catuvellauni as the most advanced and capable tribal community in Britain. By honouring their cantonal capital they were, in a limited symbolic sense, restored to their former overlordship. But if the Romans showed a high degree of statemanship in their handling of the Catuvellauni, they signally failed with the Iceni, and all this burgeoning forth of town life, trading and civic dignity were swept away at a stroke when in AD 60 Boudicca's host, having sacked Camulodunum and Londinium, destroyed Verulamium too, and with all the horrors of fire and slaughter extinguished its life, thus revenging themselves on those Britons who had come to terms with Rome.

Early in the 1930s Dr (later Sir) Mortimer Wheeler and Mrs Tessa Wheeler made a brilliantly stimulating study of Verulamium, but we knew very little of this first Roman town until Professor Sheppard Frere conducted a series of excavations from 1955 to 1961 which greatly extended our knowledge. In 1955 a first-century defensive ditch and bank

was discovered; it enclosed three sides of the town rectangle, leaving the fourth open but covered by the marshes of the River Ver. Traces of the street grid have also been detected supplementing Watling Street, whose awkward diagonal, due to the Claudian fort, remained to give a special character to the town, which measured approximately 3,000 by 2,000 feet. The dating of this defensive ditch and bank (no doubt with the usual palisade) is a matter of some difficulty, but that it was pre-Boudiccan is considered likely. It has often been suggested that Boudicca selected Camulodunum, Londinium and Verulamium as major victims for assault because they had no defences, but this is, in fact, a misreading of Tacitus, who wrote that the Iceni avoided 'forts and military posts', which is not quite the same thing. By AD 60 the Claudian fort at Verulamium had certainly been engulfed by the new town, and its garrison evacuated.

Traces of Roman pre-Boudiccan buildings, all of timber, have been found, notably a row of ships connected by a colonnade fronting on Watling street. They were all starkly functional in form, but to the Belgic townspeople they were as revolutionary as the glass and steel office blocks were to people of our own day. The planning and workmanship shows the hand of the military engineer, and these colonnades and shops and timber houses, not less than the infilling of Belgic huts with their thatched roofs, only needed the Iceni torches to start a totally consuming enormous bonfire. Coin and pottery evidence indicate that the rebuilding was very slow, and it would seem that Verulamium was derelict for 15–20 years: then in AD 79 the new Forum and Basilica, this time of brick and stone, were dedicated, according to the interpretation of fragments of the dedicatory inscription which were found in 1955. This was the time of Agricola's cultural drive, when the Britons were induced by various means to take their place in a civilising force which had turned from war to peace. The new buildings at Verulamium were designed and constructed by civilians, and were less stark than their predecessors, but, of course, were generally timber and daub, probably very like medieval work. A large market-hall, very much the Roman version of a supermarket, was built on Watling Street, and a substantial Celtic-type temple, stone built, now appeared, and the Triangular Temple was built a little later. The useless defensive bank and ditch, a sombre reminder, were levelled and filled in, to make way for new streets and buildings. In 155 a great fire devastated more than 52 acres of buildings, that is, rather more than a quarter of the town, but the momentum of nearly eighty years prosperity allowed no interval such as had occurred after AD 60. There was replanning of certain streets, and two new temples were added to the one already in being along the south-west side of the Forum: the Theatre, connected by a new street with the north-west angle of the Forum, was built, and large new stone houses for the local nobility gave diversity to the architectural form of the town. These second-century houses were of some splendour, and painted wall decorations of great delicacy have been found – in surprisingly large fragments. It is interesting to compare these essentially Classical – that is, stylistically Mediterranean – works with the third-century gorgeous but crude works which also have been discovered. Splendid second- and third-century mosaics have also survived in almost perfect condition.

Towards the end of the second century the town was walled, although that is in a sense a misstatement, since the 'wall' must have been an earthen bank protected by a ditch. The only portion of this work which has survived lies to the north and west outside the later town wall, and is known as the Fosse. It has two arms, one pointing towards the river, and the other, apparently, towards the London Gate. But the scheme was never completed and we do not know why. It is considered likely that the two great London and Chester Gates were also built at this time, and it is a mystery why these two somewhat extravagant structures, with their half-round towers, double carriage-ways and foot-ways, and measuring 100 feet across, should have been left isolated, and of only monumental value at a time when the effective fortification of British towns must have been ordered by the central authority. In 193, Septimius Severus became Emperor, defeated Albinus, Governor of Britain, and, as well as ruthlessly reorganising the administration of the Province and re-establishing the frontier, initiated a spate of building activity: it was probably at this time that the stone town-walls of Verulamium came into being. For the first time the town was walled on all sides, for the River Ver had been tamed and canalised, and the once protective marshes were no longer of defensive value. The great Gates were incorporated into the defences, and lost their air of being stranded monsters, the triangle to the north-west enclosed by the Fosse earthwork was abandoned, and was compensated for by the inclusion of a somewhat smaller area to the south-west. The Roman town had reached its final phase, and its shape was now rigidly held in the straight-jacket of its walls. Perhaps nostalgically, the limits of the old late Antonine town were commemorated by the erection of two monumental arches, both on Watling Street: one at a point 100 feet south of the Triangular Temple and the other halfway between the Theatre and the Chester Gate, where, incidentally, excavation has disclosed underlying conduits and an arched sewer. It is thought that they had dual carriage-ways, with a central pier, and measured approximately 85 feet in width. A third monumental arch was built across Watling Street at a later date, possibly around 300: it was immediately adjacent to the Theatre.

In the third century (and this has been referred to elsewhere) the Empire was nearly torn apart by endless civil wars, a rapid succession of weak emperors and the consequential weakening of authority. There was the looming threat of barbarian aggression. Economic stringency, due to a variety of reasons, led to high taxation, and that led to a curtailment of building and public spending: nowhere could this have been more marked than in Verulamium, where there is no evidence of building in this desolate time – except the town-walls, in the early spate of Severan activity. Only when Constantius restored authority did the pendulum swing back again, and prosperity return. The Theatre was restored and even enlarged, and there was much other rebuilding and reconstruction. But changes were taking place, and it has been noted that on temple sites, after a mid-century short-lived Pagan revival, coin finds show a marked decrease; this has been linked with the rise of Christianity. The Temple connected with the Theatre closed its entrance gate leading thereto, a sign of the severance between the two establishments; at the same time, the Theatre finally went out of use and it was used as a rubbish dump for the Forum, probably due to Christian disapproval. But the town prospered, and continued to do so well into the fifth century. At least one fine mansion was erected as late as 370, and later still, c. 380–390, two of its main rooms were enlarged and floored with fine new mosaics. And in the middle of the century there was still sufficient vitality – and money – to make it possible to add new-style bastions and towers to the south wall. No other Roman town in Britain has such a well-recorded history of the fifth century. In 429, Bishop Germanus of Auxerre visited Verulamium, and, according to a near-contemporary account, went in procession to the tomb of the proto-martyr St Alban, and was attended by a multitude of people, and magistrates and a man of tribunician rank, all in splendid apparel. He again visited the town in 447 (he came to Britain on both occasions for 'religious disputation'). The good bishop was asked to lead a force against the Picts, so he assumed command of the Britons, organised an ambush, and with the unlikely battle-cry of 'Alleluia' attacked and destroyed the barbarians at a site traditionally in the Welsh Marches. Despite this disturbing interlude, Verulamium was still, evidently, a suitable place for civilised discussion. Bede, the Saxon chronicler, described the martyrdom of Saint Alban: he speaks of the procession going over the bridge, at St Michael's, to the hill top (where the great Cathedral stands today) and there in the 'arena' he gave his life for his faith. Topographically, the description is exactly right, and there is no reason to doubt the authenticity of the story. Geoffrey of Monmouth – not perhaps the most reliable of historians – relates that Verulamium was held by the Saxons at the end of the fifth century, and a battle was fought with the Britons led by Uther Pendragon. By the eleventh century the Roman town had become a quarry, and not only a quarry, but according to an account preserved by Matthew Paris, the ruins had become 'the hiding places of robbers, body-snatchers and evil women'. Spoliation has continued through the ages to the present day with the construction of a new arterial road across the site.

THE FORUM

The Verulamium Forum differed from the simple Silchester, Caerwent type because of three temple-like structures arranged along the south-east to north-west side; two of these are visible in the drawing. They extended across the 26-feet wide early second-century ambulatory, of which fragments have been found, including a centrally placed massive street entrance on the east side at right angles to the Basilica on the north-east, and the three temples on the opposite side of the 305 by 200 feet space of the Forum contained by the ambulatories. The remarkable structure with the pyramidal roof on the right centre of the drawing has been dated as late second century. It has been suggested that, because of its disproportionally heavy construction, it was designed to carry a barrel vault of at least 20 feet in height. Inside there was a criss-cross of strengthening walls, and the eight-foot thick side walls had external square projections, which may have carried free-standing columns. Fundamentally, the plan of this unique building was square, with an extension covering the Forum ambulatory, and a square-sided apsidal north end. It is considered possible, even probable, that these massive foundations indicate a podium designed to support a towering monument such as is indicated in the drawing. The Forum facades of the three temples have been found to be almost exactly similar in plan, and it is reasonable to think that these buildings were harmonious in design with classical type colonnaded faca-des with the usual triangular pediments and entablatures.

The Forum, dominated by the Basilica on the one side and the three temples on the other, with monumental street entrances to the right and the left, must have been, architecturally, extremely impressive. The open space within the ambulatories was the equivalent to the Italian piazza or the English market-square, though the latter is seldom so concentrated, or formal in design. The column surmounted by the statue of Victory has no archaeological authority in this instance, but it was not unusual to ornament public areas in this way (cf. Colchester) and there is every reason to suppose that the human activities as shown were normal in such a setting. Reconstructions of Roman life very often suffer from a 'blanched' look, but all the evidence points to the use of crude and bright colour in the clothing of both sexes, and it has been said that the northern peoples were 'especially colour-conscious'. In Verulamium this would be in accord with the brilliant and powerful wall paintings in the houses. Use was also made of chequer patterning and striped materials. We know that the Gauls were masters of dyeing techniques, and it would be surprising if their close relatives in Britain were without these same tastes and talents.

THE TRIANGULAR TEMPLE

The street grid at a point 700 feet from the (not yet built) South-east Gate impinged on the already existing diagonal line of Watling Street, and an awkward triangle resulted from this convergence. The position was an important one: a busy main-road junction where there was appearing something of the character of a ceremonial way, and within a hundred feet of the triangular site a triumphal arch was soon to be built over Watling Street, the Londinium road. A temple, it seems, was chosen in the early second century as a structure sufficiently significant functionally and aesthetically for such prominence. The shape of temple and courtyard was, inevitably, a truncated triangle with the temple standing transversely across its broader end or base.

It was divided into three compartments or cells, of which the central and most holy, was a self-contained unit, separated from the other two by a wide corridor, and contained the statue of the god – the imprint of the red and yellow painted pedestal was found by the excavator. In the two side cells were pits or tanks centrally placed, which may have been used for burnt offerings, since oak charcoal was found in them. There were no less than fifteen of these small pits in the floors of the temple and courtyard, all containing calcined bones of animals, oak charcoal and pottery, and in at least two of them were deposits of charred seeds and scales from Italian pine cones. All these, no doubt, were connected with votive offerings. The floor of the courtyard was slightly lower than that of the temple, perhaps to avoid the risk of rainwater flooding.

There were three structural phases in the history of the Temple, and in the final phase a central altar had been inserted in the courtyard flooring (which at an earlier stage had been of rammed gravel but had deteriorated to inferior cement patched with brick) and flanked on either side by smaller pedestals: behind it an ox skull had been found buried, and this is thought to have been connected with the re-dedication of the temple, after what was probably an extensive restoration at the time of the Constantinian revival. But before this, in the first half of the second century, a serious subsidence occurred, due to the faulty filling of the underlying ditch which had run parallel to Watling Street. Not only the Temple, but the colonnades surrounding the courtyard were affected, probably a number of the 14–16 feet high columns had to be renewed, as well as the massive central piers on the north side which flanked the entrance to the *cella* of the temple itself. At this time too, the external timber porch was added, and the high surrounding walls were faced with crimson-coloured plaster. Twenty feet south of the porch, and on the same axis there stood, it is supposed, a large external altar whose chalk foundation has been noted. Wooden posts, at five foot intervals along three sides of the temple complex, protected the walls from damage, and although post holes have not been found to extend as far as the altar, it is easy to imagine this part of the street as being a gathering place for worshippers and for ceremonial use.

The nature of the votive offerings give some clue to the dedication of the temple, especially the pine-seeds, which must have been imported from Italy at great cost. They were an offering associated with the worship of the Phrygian Cybele, the 'Great Mother', the goddess of human progress, and the patroness of cities. In art she was represented as wearing a diadem of towers: no site in Verulamium could have been more appropriate for her shrine.

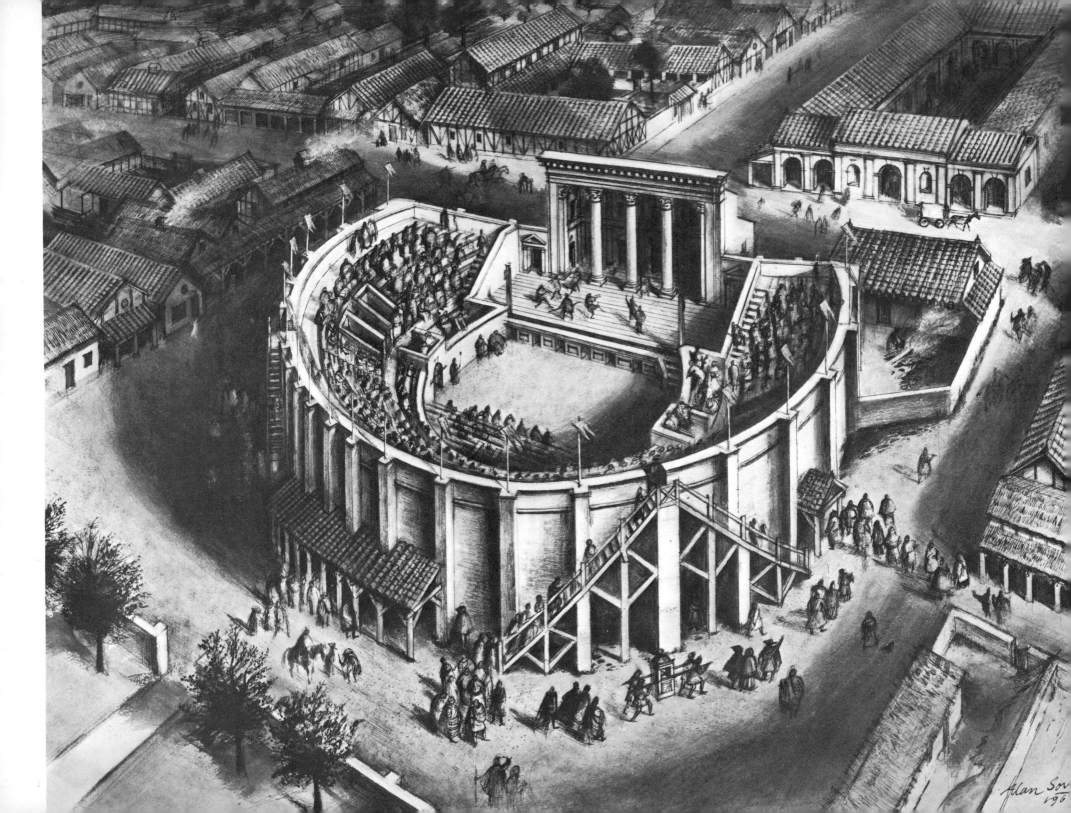

THE THEATRE

Few indications of Romano-British theatres have been found, and the theatre at Verulamium is the only instance where the complete plan has survived and has been excavated and recorded, and this study is of great interest because it not only elucidates problems of design and construction, but also demonstrates changes and developments over a period of 250 years. The Theatre was built *c.* AD 155, soon after a disastrous fire had destroyed much of the town, and as no signs of earlier buildings have been found on the site it is thought that the site had been reserved for it. Theatres were used for religious ceremonies as well as for entertainments of all kinds. This theatre was on the same axis as, and connected with, the Romano-Celtic type temple to the south. This becomes clearer when the form of the First Period theatre is considered, for it bore a distinct likeness to an amphitheatre with the orchestra (that is, the central area enclosed by the cavea and its tiers of seats) planned as a circular arena and the focal point for the audience, rather than the stage, which was small and whose curved front wall was bounded by the arena wall. Backstage there was a small dressing-room. Sir Mortimer Wheeler has described this circular orchestra type as the 'cockpit theatre'. He notes that twenty or more examples have been found in Gaul, mostly in the north, and links them with the Gallo-Roman or Romano-Celtic temple as a 'manifestation of . . . provincial individuality'. The outer, supporting wall of the whole theatre structure was perhaps 25 feet high, strengthened with buttresses, and between this and the arena wall was a filling of gravel on which were laid wooden seats, which were reached by external and internal wooden stairs. Access to the arena-orchestra was through three vaulted tunnels beneath the cavea.

Very soon – *c.*AD 160 – this cockpit-theatre was so altered that it became close to the normal type of Roman theatre: the stage front was now straightened so that it projected into the orchestra, one half of which was covered with a timber staging supported by massive timber uprights, and the low seats on this platform became orchestra stalls. The stage itself was embellished with a row of Corinthian columns 19 feet high, with, no doubt, the appropriate entablature and the architectural background and exits similar to those which are still to be seen at Orange, Sabratha and Aspendos. Forty years later, in AD 200, an earlier mechanism had been replaced by a double masonry wall along the front of the stage, and in the slot between them had been housed the curtain. At both ends of this slot were vertical posts with counterweights for raising and lowering this theatrical necessity: one of these counterweights has survived. These later developments all point to continued prosperity and vitality, but from the middle of the third century economic and political conditions in the empire became so serious that prosperity departed, towns became ruinous and public buildings were allowed to fall into disrepair. So the Verulamium Theatre became a wreck until, with the re-establishment of the central authority by Constantius in 296, a new and vigorous age began. The Theatre was repaired and enlarged by the construction of very massive outer walls of the auditorium. The external staircases were demolished, the seating area was increased in size, the orchestra was altered in shape, the wooden staging was removed and it seems possible that it was once again used for shows in conjunction with the stage. The rooms adjoining the stage were rebuilt, and at this time a triumphal arch was constructed over the nearby Watling Street. (These Constantinian developments are not shown in the drawing, which can be dated *c.* 200.)

The Theatre continued in use until *c.* 380, and then it seems to have been abandoned and become a rubbish dump. It is remarkable that a great public building in the centre of a still prosperous town should have been treated in this contemptuous way, and it has been suggested that Christian disapproval of ritual and ceremonies connected with pagan cults may have been responsible.

Colchester (Camulodunum)

The immediate objective of Claudius in Britain was Camulodunum, the capital of the Belgic kingdom which extended over south-eastern Britain, and whose ruler Cunobelin was styled by Suetonius as REX BRITANNORUM. The turmoil which ensued after his death in AD 40 provided the Romans with an opportunity, even an excuse, for their long-expected invasion. The name Camulodunum means 'The Strong Place of Camulos' – a war-god – not perhaps an entirely happy augury, but the Romans had no premonitions of disaster and Camulodunum it remained. This Belgic city, if such it can be called, was by no means the close-knit Mediterranean concept familiar to the Romans, but a wide area of diffused building and cultivation, with a greater concentration of habitation lying to the north-west of the later Roman town. It was protected on the north and east by the River Colne, and on the south by the River Roman, and on the west the gap between the rivers was defended by three successive lines of immense earthworks and ditches. These would have been more than adequate against any British attack, but were of no avail against the disciplined valour of the legions, and Claudius was able to act the part of the great conqueror with the minimum of delay.

At the time of the conquest Camulodunum was accepted without question as the capital of the newly formed Province and, in fact, its position was not unfavourable for trade and communication with the Continent. But it was totally unsuitable as the focal point of the road system which rapidly came into being, and the upstart Londinium, at the very centre of the web, very soon became the capital, in fact if not in name.

A legionary fortress, symbol of domination, was established at Camulodunum, where modern Colchester now stands, and it was garrisoned by Legion XX for some years, until the forward thrust of the legions to the west, demanding more and still more troops for the war frontier, and the deceptive peace in the south-east, caused the Romans to evacuate it. Although this policy later was seen to have been a disastrous one, the immediate compensation offered prosperity and even splendour. For the Emperor Claudius, mindful perhaps of his triumph, decreed that Camulodunum should become a *colonia*, the first in Britain, and be called *Colonia Claudia Victricensis* in his honour. And further, it was to be the headquarters of the Imperial Cult, with a great Temple of Claudius, and a College of Priests. The site chosen was the whale-back hill just south of the Colne and south-east of the old Belgic city, and its alignment was exactly east and west. Surprisingly, there is no evidence of any pre-Roman use of the site, but it has now been established that the legionary fortress occupied its western end. The time-expired veterans were given plots of land requisitioned from the native owners, and were responsible for the development of the town, and, ominously, for defence. For the next eleven years there was unprecedented activity: the great Temple of the Divine Claudius was built, as were the College of Priests, the Senate House and Forum, Public Baths, a Theatre, and, of course, houses, shops and warehouses. But the Britons, toiling in forced labour-gangs, taxed outrageously and treated with irresponsible brutality, found that they had merely exchanged their Belgic overlords for the Roman. In these tumultuous days following the conquest rapacious Roman financiers moved in, lent money at extortionate rates of interest, then suddenly foreclosed, threatening violence if repayment was delayed: Seneca and even Claudius are mentioned in this connection. The huge Temple was seen as an expression of eternal servitude: the Britons, of course, had to pay for the annual rites and festivities, shows, games and literary and musical contests. The Romans, in their arrogant self-confidence, had built no fortifications, and when Boudicca, widowed Queen of the neighbouring Iceni, scourged and insulted beyond endurance, rose in revolt, Camulodunum was her first objective. The veterans, defending their only strong point, the Temple of Claudius, were overwhelmed, and in a terrible two days' sack the town and everything in it was destroyed, as were Londinium and Verulamium. It was an orgy of torture and massacre. The Governor Suetonius Paullinus with the legions was far away destroying the Druids' sanctuary in Anglesey, and he could not save but only avenge. This was in AD 60. When the Roman power was reasserted it was unthinkable that a burnt-out town and ruined temple could remain as a permanent scar, so what we may describe as Camulodunum II came into being, and all the surviving fragments, with the exception of the Temple foundations, are from this rebuilding.

The new town was an oblong of 108 acres divided into 40 *insulae* in which there is some diversity of size and shape, though they all conform to a rectangular pattern. After the terrible experience of the Boudiccan sack one might reasonably assume that the new town had defences at an early date but, like those of the other towns of the province, they belong to the late second century: much of the wall is standing to nearly its original height of about 18 feet, including the merlons. The wall was backed by an earthen rampart, and in front there was a 20-feet wide ditch which was obliterated by a medieval cutting. The construction was massive: the wall was eight feet, eight inches thick at the base, with a rubble and concrete core, faced with squared septaria, that is, flint nodules from London clay, with quadrupled courses of brick. Of the gateways, only fragments of the splendid West or Balkerne Gate survive, with its two carriageways and two footways. The East Gate, which may have been similar in design, was demolished as late as 1675, after one of those dismal municipal confabulations, in which Mayor, Aldermen and Chamberlain pondered, and inevitably destroyed. These two monumental structures were at either end of the main street, now the High Street of modern Colchester: from the west ran the road through Braintree, Great Dunmow and Bishop's Stortford to St Albans and the Midlands, while another went through Chelmsford to London. To the east, and this demonstrates the lop-sided position of the town, the road led only to the Hythe, the harbour on the Colne. There were probably six other smaller gates along the north and south

walls, and two important roads went from them into East Anglia. Traces of square internal turrets have come to light where the town streets touch the wall, but there were no external bastions in Roman times – those visible today date from the fourteenth century when there was extensive repair work done to the fortifications. This lack of Roman bastions is remarkable, especially bearing in mind the exposed position of Camulodunum and its strategic importance. Was the town so confident in the strength of its outmoded system of fortification that it could ignore the new method with its superior (and economical) capacity for flanking fire? Of course, the Balkerne Gate must in itself have served as a projecting bastion on the west wall, and there may have been something similar on the east, but what of the much longer north and south walls? Perhaps the defenders were content to trust to marshy land. But nevertheless the absence of bastions is puzzling – and evidently the medieval engineers thought them necessary along the south wall.

It is unlikely that the rebuilt Temple would be dedicated to the murdered Claudius by Nero, but the Imperial Cult remained. Here was no Romano-British four-square temple, but a great classical building, which would not have been out of place in Rome itself. It was set in a vast courtyard measuring 350 feet from east to west and 450 feet from north to south. It was raised on a podium, a masonry platform 11 feet high above ground level and 13 feet below, and its length was 105 feet and width 85 feet. The facade, facing south, had a double line of eight Corinthian columns, and eleven along the east and west sides: each column had a diameter of 3 feet, 6 inches and was 30 feet high. It was decorated with marble from the Mediterranean lands, and it is probable that the triangular pediment was embellished with sculpture, gilded and coloured. From courtyard level to the colonnade was a wide flight of steps, and in front of them was a great altar flanked by pedestals that once supported statues: maybe the statue of Victory, which Tacitus mentions as having fallen and 'turned its back on the enemy as though it fled before them', was one of these. Because of the shortage of building stone in Essex all this weight and magnificence was carried, not on solid masonry foundations, but on two parallel vaults which were filled with rammed earth. Long after the destruction of the Temple – and we do not know when this occurred – the Normans built their castle on and around the podium, which they probably assumed to be solid masonry, and it was not until 1683 when a certain John Weeley tried, unsuccessfully, to demolish the castle, that the vaults were discovered, and then they were not identified until in 1919 Mortimer Wheeler and P. G. Laver published a paper demonstrating the astonishing facts of this piece of unwitting conservation by the Norman castle builders.

The temple courtyard was enclosed on all sides by colonnades and administrative buildings, and on the south side there is evidence of a monumental entrance and screen wall. The two ends of this screen wall may have been linked by arched gateways to the wall on the south side of the street, which may well have been that of the priestly college. The fact that Camulodunum has been constantly rebuilt, in Saxon, Norman, Medieval, Tudor, Georgian and Victorian times, and (probably most destructive of all) in our own day, explains why it is that, comparatively, so little of Roman Colchester has survived. On the other hand objects found have been prodigious in both quantity and quality. An L-shaped building which has been thought to have been a *mithraeum* has been excavated to the east of the Temple, but its purpose remains conjectural, and what were, perhaps, houses of the courtyard type, to the north, have been noted, as have scattered fragments elsewhere. To the west of the Temple, with its south frontage on the High Street, and occupying the site of the legionary fortress, there may have stood the Basilica and Forum, the focal point of the civil administration of the *colonia*. Tacitus refers to the Theatre and a Senate House in the pre-Boudiccan town: Senate House could be equated with Basilica, and the modern street plan of the area adjacent to Northgate Street shows something very suggestive of a Theatre site – a plan of 1610 emphasises this with special clarity.

Camulodunum, like Lincoln, another *colonia*, had a splendid drainage system, and an impressive section of it, stone-built and tile-vaulted, with a clearance of five feet runs north from the so-called *mithraeum* mentioned above, and had its outfall at the North-East Gate: the town with the ground falling away on all sides, was, of course, ideal for drainage purposes, and the site was selected for that, no doubt, amongst other reasons. The cemeteries were extensive, and more than 700 graves have been recorded. They were located outside the walls, with concentrations to the south-west and north. It is noteworthy that while no remains of Romano-British type temples have been found within the walls, not less than five, and probably more, have been discovered to the north-west and west, where the British pre-Roman town once stood. There too have been found numerous pottery kilns, and we may reasonably assume that a large industrial suburb, lacking the amenities of the Roman town, but thriving nevertheless, continued to exist there from the earliest times. We do know that the only centre for samian ware in Britain was established here in the late second century.

Around Camulodunum there is woven a legendary tale that is both shadowy and grandiose: it is the tale of King Coel and his daughter, Helena, Constantius, and their son, the great Constantine. The legend is recorded in the Colchester Oath Book of the fourteenth century. The prosaic, and generally accepted historical tale is that Helena was born in Bithynia, and that Constantine was born at Naissus in Dardania. But where there is a tenacious folk-story it is foolish to dismiss it too easily as a fairy-story. Perhaps Helena was a British princess and her father King of Camulodunum. In our own time Eveln Waugh has embroidered the tale very charmingly in his *Helena* and makes the past live again.

It is (as with all towns in Roman Britain) difficult to estimate the population within the walls, but at Camulo-dunum 7,500 souls may not be wide of the mark. We do not know how the Roman town ended its life, but large areas of burning, and the evidence of burning brushwood piled against one of the gates, all point to violence and disaster. Very likely the town was attacked and partly destroyed in those blank years that followed the end of Roman rule, but we know the town walls were repaired in late Saxon times, which means there was much to defend and preserve, and continuous, if partial, occupation, is in fact more reasonable a supposition than total desertion.

THE BALKERNE GATE

This monumental structure was the west gate of the Roman town: it might have been called, from the direction of the road which led through it, the London Gate, but it has been known as the Balkerne or Balcon from the earliest times, though the reason for this is obscure. It stands where the hill begins to descend steeply towards the north and the remains are more substantial than those of any other Roman town gate in Britain, even though they are partly built over by the King's Head Inn and caged in by a hideous iron grill. The gate measured 107 feet from north to south, and 39 feet from east to west. There were four portals – two carriageways and two footways – and it is remarkable that the archway of the south footway and of the adjoining guard room still survive intact, and the north tower still rises to 20 of its original 40 feet. The construction and materials of the gate are similar to that of the town-wall, that is, rubble and mortar core, with a facing of squared septaria alternating with brick courses. The centre part of the gate with the twin portals was originally a monumental arch quite independent of any defences, belonging, perhaps, to the reconstruction of the *colonia* after the holocaust of AD 60. The arch was incorporated into the gate when the defences were built at this end of the second century. Excavation has produced interesting evidence which shows that at some time during the Roman period the gate fell into ruin and its subsequent rebuilding reduced the width of the carriageways from

seventeen to ten feet. Finally, it was devastated by fire, perhaps at the hands of the Saxons. But the immensely strong masonry shell must have survived, for at a later date, and usually associated with the repairs made to the walls by Edward the Elder in 917, the north footway and the two carriageways were blocked by a wall of barbarously crude workmanship; it was then that the London road was realigned to enter the town at Head Gate.

SOUTH FACADE OF THE TEMPLE COURT

This may have been one of the comparatively few architectural compositions of what might be described as the conventional classical pattern to be found in Roman Britain, and the special reason for this at Camulodunum was, of course, that it should enhance the grandeur of the headquarters of the Imperial Cult, of which the Temple of Claudius was the focal point. Massive foundations have been discovered on the north side of the modern High Street which indicate a monumental entrance to the Temple Court, directly in line with the centre of the Temple facade and the great altar. Until the coming of the Normans a good deal of this must have been visible above ground, but they piled their earth rampart over the solid stone platform measuring 28 by 26 feet with a large portion of its west wall standing to a height of 8 feet, and a fragment of a part-engaged column faced with red plaster – all this had been preserved by the castle rampart. A series of piers slightly varying in size from 5 feet 9 inches to 6 feet wide and with openings 6 feet 6 inches wide extended east and west from the entrance gateway and were connected by a wall which formed the rear wall of the internal arcade of the temple court. Judging from the marble fragments which have been found on the site, this monumental facade must have been extravagant in its magnificence. It is possible that the east and west ends of the street coinciding with the north-south walls of the Temple court may have been closed by structures of the triumphal-arch type linking with another colonnade on the south side of the street, which, it is reasonable to think, was the enclosing wall of a college of priests serving the temple. It is difficult to associate this kind of brightly coloured architectural splendour, and the formality of the priestly ritual, the processions and the sacrifices with the gentle and unchanging character of the Essex landscape and its enormous cloudy skies. The cost of maintaining this alien splendour must have been very great, and as it all had to be borne by the native population in the form of taxes, even the amusements, games and athletic contests, which took place annually at the time of Convention of the Province which centred on the Temple of Claudius, could not have been without a sobering counting of costs.

Lincoln (Lindum Colonia)

Lincoln, the Roman Lindum *colonia*, is remarkable for its dramatic siting on an isolated plateau sloping down to the River Witham. The name Lindum derives from the British *lindos*, meaning 'marsh' or 'lake', still valid as a description of the marshes of the Witham which to this day survive within sight of the city. Lindum, one of the four *coloniae* in Britain, began as a legionary fortress garrisoned by the ninth and second legions successively and was established *c.* AD 65, although there was probably a smaller fort there *c.*AD 50. It has aptly been described as a 'bastion' for it was a key-point in the first Roman frontier which was established between the Severn and Trent in those years of conquest. It protected the new province from the north, and from its strange natural position, the garrison could at the same time overawe the Brigantes to the north, guard the crossing of the Trent at Littleborough and stand sentinel over the south, where were, as events were to show, the unreliable allies, the Iceni of Norfolk. The defences of the legionary fortress were erected in two stages: the first was a timber-faced clay rampart on a layer of broken rock, protected by a 15-foot wide ditch. One ditch only has been found, but it may have formed part of a multiple system later submerged in the great ditch of the Roman town. Stage two in the legionary fortress defences was the addition of towers and a fireproof sloping front as well as a new ditch or ditches. These changes probably occurred very soon after the original defences were built and then, in the reign of Domitian, the *colonia* was founded, superseding the legionary fortress and the military rampart was given a stone front. Fortress and *colonia* occupied the same site. A *colonia* needed cultivable lands for the veterans turned farmers, and at Lindum there were the rich lands on the limestone plateau and marshy areas, which could be drained and whose development into the typical Italianate chequerboard pattern of fields was so different from the sprawling irregularity of the typical native Celtic fields, but which has left no recognisable trace in Britain. Probably there would be little disturbance caused to the Coritani by this agricultural development, and a

curious sidelight has been thrown on the Roman way of arranging such matters, by our knowledge that under Domitian, compensation was paid for disturbance of crops and it is possible that land taken over for the *colonia* was paid for. Such behaviour to the Trinovantes some years earlier would certainly have prevented a great disaster and saved thousands of lives.

Building on the steep slope below the hill-top plateau must have started during the military occupation, but there is evidence of pre-Roman occupation by the river which spread up the hill. The legionary presence would have attracted a considerable civil community and use would have been made of the river for bringing in heavy supplies and wharfs constructed. The fortress too would have had its *canabae*, an area round one of the main gates and under military control, where the wine shops and brothels would be found. The area on the slope between the fortress/*colonia* and the river was fortified during the troubles at the end of the second century with all the other towns of the province; the upper area, however, had a stone wall added to the front of the old legionary rampart at an earlier date, probably in the first half of the second century, but the precise date is still in dispute. There was further rebuilding, it is thought, in the third century and the final stage was probably at the end of the fourth.

Lincoln is unique in having part of a Roman gate, the Newport arch, that is in use, although it suffered serious damage in 1964, when a large lorry laden with frozen fish fingers from Grimsby tried to get through it. A fragment of the east gate can be seen in front of the Eastgate Hotel, and a very fine gate has been found and excavated on the west side of the extended defences in the Park where the new local government offices now stand. This gate with its large square projecting towers dates from the fourth century and was perhaps the work of Theodosius, since it contains re-used moulded stones from monuments probably demolished for this purpose. At the same time, the old stone wall was thickened and strengthened where it had become weakened with age. Some of the concrete core of this late wall can be seen to the east of the Newport arch. Everywhere inside the walled areas buildings have been found, and this also can be said of a suburb to the east, and there was a long straggling development along the main road to the south. The most substantial buildings so far discovered have been in the upper *colonia*, and include a large bath-house and the central complex which had an elaborate colonnade along Bailgate, and a length of plain wall known as the Mint Wall is still standing to a height of 18 feet. One interesting feature of Lincoln was its water supply brought in from a stream known as the Roaring Meg, over a mile to the north-east. Normally this would have been by gravity, but in this case the water had to be raised against a 60-foot head by a pump at the source. The earthenware pipes encased in waterproof concrete, pieces of which can be seen in the Museum, discharged the water into a tank in the north-east corner of the upper *colonia*, and from there it flowed freely into the rest of the town and a public fountain was found near the Stonebow some years ago. A very fine sewer was discovered in Bailgate in the nineteenth century, large enough for a man to walk down it and with junctions from houses and streets. There were the usual extensive cemeteries on all sides and some large pottery works which were very active in the fourth century, producing ware with a chocolate slip with white painted decoration. A visit to the Museum, which is unsuitably housed in a medieval building, will give a glimpse of the wealth of the Roman city in the few fragments of fine sculpture and metalwork which have survived.

Silchester (Calleva Atrebatum)

Silchester, known to the Romano-Britons as Calleva Atrebatum, 'The Woodland Town', was encompassed by forests, traces of which remain to this day. It lies ten miles south of Reading, but the visitor, knowing its fame and expecting much, may be disappointed to find that the only visible remains of the Roman town are the massive and remarkably well-preserved stretches of the town wall, which enclose corn fields, a medieval church and some farm buildings. Silchester is the only Romano-British town the whole area of which has been excavated, although only the uppermost buildings revealed, but after a wonderful booty of objects of all kinds, including pavements, had been extracted from the site, the architectural remains were reinterred in their ancient grave, because it was found that exposure to the elements was causing deterioration which threatened total loss. Archaeological operations began in a methodical way as long ago as 1744 when the cobbler-yeoman John Stair, by observing the crop-marks in a hot summer, was able to lay bare the Roman street-grid. He also discovered what he quite rightly called 'The Market Place' – the Forum – and excavated several houses, and then, in association with a surveyor named Wright, produced an excellently accurate plan of the irregular but balanced octagon of about 107 acres which was the Roman walled town. The site is almost level, and the town stood on a gravel plateau, or spur, with the ground sloping away on the north, south and east sides, whilst to the west and north-west the land was slightly more level. But the country is so gently undulating and without dramatic characteristics, that one is apt to see the wall-enclosed fields as merely a continuation of what lies outside.

The great period of excavation began in 1864, with the enthusiastic cooperation and interest of the second Duke of Wellington, the owner of the site, and has gone on intermittently ever since. Not surprisingly, interest was concentrated on the Roman walled town until early in this century when the Belgic foundation began to receive increasing attention. We now know that there was an *oppidum* – a defended settlement – on the Silchester site, and

that it was the capital of the Atrebates, a Belgic tribe which, under their chief Commius, had fled before the victorious Caesar from Gaul about 50 BC. The refugees rapidly assumed the role of conquerors in southern Britain, and gained control of a large area of Hampshire and the adjacent counties. Commius probably died about 20 BC and the Belgic ditch and earthwork defences at Calleva have been dated at the end of the period BC, and enclosed an area of 90 acres. In AD 44–45 the legions commanded by Vespasian sweeping south westwards may have occupied Calleva, but we do not know whether it was one of the twenty *oppida* which his biographer claims were stormed by him. It is unlikely, for why should the Celtic population have supported their Belgic overlords in any martial action? The Roman strategists evidently approved the siting of what was to become the 'nodal point' (as it has been called) of their spider-web of roads in southern Britain, so the Roman town superseded the Belgic *oppidum*. What is now known as the First Roman defence, or the Outer Earthwork, enclosed 230 acres, and it is thought to be of first century date. It is impossible to say with any degree of certainty why it should have been considered necessary to construct such large-scale defensive works – the ditch was 40 feet wide and 10 feet deep and the bank perhaps 30 feet high topped with a palisade. These defences, three generations after the conquest, can only have been against enemies of the *Pax Romana,* and one authority suggests that the threat may have come from Wales, though the idea that the Welsh tribes at that, or any other, time could have threatened the heartland of Roman Britain seems to carry an overtone of fantasy. Another suggestion is that these earthworks were a demarcation line, in the manner of the Hadrian's Wall *vallum,* but the scale of the ditch and embankment is against that: we may never know the reason. The last thing the Romans wanted, of course, was the revival of British *oppida*, so this must have been a delicate matter of policy. The only tactically weak point, the north-west, was protected by a salient (known as 'The Annexe' which, incidentally, cut through a Belgic

defensive work which has been compared with the long dykes at Camulodunum).

The street plan has been dated to the early second century and there are indications that it was executed as a single unit. A marked characteristic of Calleva appears to have been the high proportion of open space within the walls, and in our own day it has been referred to as 'The Garden Town'. However, it must be borne in mind that the town was excavated in the nineteenth century, when there was not nearly such acute attention paid to the possibility of post-holes and other indications of timber buildings as there is today. Therefore, some of the empty spaces which occur in the excavations were very likely occupied by timber buildings or robbed out stone foundations which were not recognised by the excavators at that time.

The Forum and Basilica and about one hundred structures conflict with the right-angled rigidity of the street grid, and one may assume that they were in being before the street grid was made, and these were survivors of the so-called Old Town of the first century. Not all was improvement: for instance, the Public Baths originally had a fine entrance portico 65 feet long with eight Tuscan columns of Bath stone, and it was found that these columns were not only out of alignment with the new road but actually projected five feet into it, so they were cut down and their stumps have been found buried beneath the ancient roadway. So it would seem that things have not changed very much in historical times, and that Bumbledom and Town Planners (fatal combination) have always put 'The Scheme' before flexibility and amenity. The Baths and other nearby eccentrically sited buildings were near the banks of a stream which supplied water to the Baths and coped with the drainage: the stream still flows on. Unquestionably, the largest, functionally the most important, and visually the most impressive building complex in Calleva was the Basilica and Forum. Like so much in the town (and this applies, in fact, to all Romano-British towns) it was military in its form and inspiration – the *principia* of a Legionary Fortress adapted to

civil usage. The complex covered nearly two acres and measured 275 feet from north to south and 313 feet from east to west, and the nave roof of the Basilica hall was 70 feet high. This great building was town-hall, council chamber (*curia*) and courts of justice – cases were tried in the apsidal tribunals at both ends, and the administrative staff of the canton worked in the offices adjoining the *curia* and in some of the rooms around the Forum, where also were shops opening into the colonnaded courtyard. A happy mixture, one might think, of bustling everyday life, the dignity of government and the terror of the law. The excavated remains of the Basilica are of two dates, for it was utterly destroyed, as will be related later, and rebuilt *c.* AD 300. Much material from the first building was re-used and repaired, but the new work was very inferior in quality, symptomatic of the declining culture. Fragments of white Italian and Pyrenean marbles and gaily coloured frescoes have been found amongst the mass of debris. One can admire the scale and grandeur of this great structure, but when in town after town the pattern is repeated with but slight variation, it becomes unexciting, and therefore, boring. Not, perhaps, until our own time, with the office-block repeated *ad infinitum* in every city in the world, has there been such evidence of architectural ossification as in the street grid and 'Basilica and Forum' of those ancient times. Of course, there were compensations, and in these loosely knit towns (not forgetting the many timber buildings which have vanished) orchards, pasture, small-holdings and courtyard gardens must have veiled the harsh rigidity of planning and the monotony of building elevations. And we should bear in mind that, in a land of untamed forest, heath and marsh, it may have been just this quality of prosaic orderliness and security which had the greatest appeal.

Five temples have been found, two of them in a sacred *temenos* which obstructed the central street from the Forum to the East Gate. Three of these temples (and there may have been a fourth where the medieval Parish Church stands) were of the usual Romano-Celtic type, with a *cella* sur-

rounded by colonnades; another was polygonal in plan, and yet another was rectangular with an apsidal end, suggestive of a *mithraeum*. To the south-east of the Basilica are the remains of what may have been a Christian church, a rarity so remarkable that it may be described as unique, (there is a note on the Christian Church on page 59). A large *mansio* or posting-station stood near the South Gate: it was very large, measuring 210 by 200 feet, and in addition had a commodious suite of baths with a sluice gate through the town-wall to carry off water and drain the latrine. It was divided into suites of rooms with hypocausts, and it is thought there was an upper storey. The *mansio* was a public building to accommodate travellers using the Imperial Post, who thus had to pay for themselves, but its maintenance fell upon the local authorities, and the arrival of some high official with a large retinue cannot have been welcomed with undiluted joy. Twenty-five large houses, about the same number of smaller ones, and a considerable number of shops, warehouses, workshops and industrial buildings of various kinds have been excavated. Dwarf walls of masonry supporting a timber structure, resembling medieval half-timbering, with mud and wattle filling, tiled roofs of the usual *tegula* and *imbrex* type or hexagonal slabs of Old Red Sandstone or Pennant Grit, or thatch, were the usual constructional materials. Where there were hypocausts, especially those which supplied heat through wall-flues, masonry or flint rubble walls up to the roof eaves would have been necessary. The question of whether there were upper floors is a vexed one, but it is difficult to see why they should not have existed. There does not appear to have been a public drainage system at Calleva, and waste disposal seems to have been dealt with by the digging of numberless pits. Generally, the larger houses were built on three sides of a courtyard with rooms opening onto external corridors.

Towards the end of the second century the town had ceased to expand, and it was clear that a more realistic defence system was desirable. If this had been a period of settled peace probably nothing would have been done, but

Commodus had been murdered, and in the struggle for supreme power Clodius Albinus, Governor of the Province, had himself proclaimed Emperor, and war against his chief rival Septimius Severus became a certainty. Even so, the logical need for these defences is difficult to grasp – unless it was the fear of a large-scale barbarian raid when the British legions were in Gaul fighting Severus (see Introduction, p. 19). In the event, what we know as the Second Roman Defence was constructed and this new ditch and bank cut off the outlying portions of the street grid. The embankment was immense – 45 feet wide and 8 feet high plus the palisade, and the ditch 22 feet wide by 7 feet deep and V-shaped in section. This earthwork became in effect the backing for the Third Roman Defence which was the Wall itself, which has been dated as early third century. It may have been considered as the final dignification of the cantonal capital rather than, at that time, for actual defence, but as the *civitates* would have borne the vast cost, that may be doubted.

It was a tremendous piece of building, of flint rubble concrete faced with dressed flints, with bonding courses of large flat slabs of Bath Stone and Forest Marble every $2\frac{1}{2}$ feet. This bonding stone came from a distance of at least 35 miles, and the prodigious cost of quarrying and transport alone can be envisaged. The wall was $9\frac{1}{2}$ feet thick at the base, on a plinth of great stones, and tapered to $7\frac{1}{2}$ feet at the top, the reduction being gained by an offset on the inside. The height was originally about 20 feet with battlements of, perhaps, 6 feet, and even today it is 15 feet high near the South Gate. The wall was backed by an earthern rampart (the Second Roman Defence) along which there was a footway, with wooden stairways leading up to the wall-walk at 200 feet intervals, where the wall was thickened sufficently to support them. No turrets or bastions have been found. The four main gates opened to the north, south, east and west, the latter pair very powerful structures with guard-rooms, and towers recessed into the wall. These had double carriageways, whilst the north and south had single portals: in

addition, there were three posterns and a sluice gate which served the *mansio*. We know nothing of the garrison of this great defence work, but obviously, it would have been absurd to construct such a costly system – paid for by the people it protected – unless an effective garrison was there to defend it. Probably in quiet times some form of militia was sufficient, with a reinforcement of tough regular troops available in emergencies. Finally, a wide ditch completed the defences: it was variable in width from 25 feet to 45 feet, and was distant from the wall by a berm of approximately 30 feet.

One other structure must be noted, the amphitheatre, outside the walls and at their north-east angle and served by a postern-gate. Earthern banks, elliptical in shape, survive to show where once was the auditorium. It has not been excavated, but it is thought that these flat-topped banks which once supported rows of wooden seats, were contained by a buttressed stone revetment, perhaps 20 feet high: a fragment still survived in 1759. The arena was about 150 by 120 feet, and here were held the games and wild beast shows, the occasional gladiatorial contest and festivals of all kinds. It can be imagined decked with banners and pennons, filled with shouting people, and then the blare of trumpets demanding silence. Today it is quiet enough, with only the occasional clucking of hens, for it is a poultry farm!

Calleva Atrebatum has no recorded history, and only the destruction of the first Basilica, already referred to, gives us a clue to the single fracturing of its life as a quiet cantonal capital. The disaster happened in AD 296, when the usurper Allectus, striving to defend the independent Imperium of Britain against the central authority of Rome, made the same kind of strategical blunder that destroyed King Harold in 1066. He rushed to meet the invasion threat from the south coast, and was decisively beaten and slain in battle. The invasion was two-pronged: Constantius, the Commander in Chief, sailed his fleet up the Thames to seize Londinium, but was delayed by fog. Meanwhile, his lieutenant, Asclepio-datus, seized the Isle of Wight, landed on the south coast

and advanced inland. Then Allectus made his miscalculation, and the campaign was over – but not for Calleva which, as the only large town in the battle area, was a natural prey to the combatants. We do not know whether it was sacked by the victors or the vanquished. Did the townsfolk open their gates, or try to defend their expensive walls – unavailingly, it would seem?

We know that Calleva was the cantonal capital, but three fragmentary inscriptions have come to light which may suggest that it became a *municipium* in later Roman times.

This was a title of honour, rather as 'city' is in our own day, and it would have given the town a precise and legal pre-eminence which 'cantonal capital' did not have. But there can be no certainty in this.

Calleva has been described, rather unkindly, as a 'failed town' because it did not continue as a town in post-Roman times. That it has not survived, even in a small way, as have, say, Alcester or Towcester, is certainly surprising when one remembers its ancient key position in a road system which is still largely in being, but the absence of a usable river may

have been crucial. But Calleva became an empty field, and so it is today.

THE CHRISTIAN CHURCH

The Christian Church at Calleva was first excavated in 1892 but reopened and studied by Sir Ian Richmond in 1961. It measures 24 by 42 feet, and is, therefore, very much smaller than any of the substantial houses and public buildings in the town. However, its size is altogether disproportionate to its importance, since it is the only Romano-British structure of basilican form which has been claimed as a Christian church. It is completely typical: narthex, nave with apsidal end and side aisles and the beginnings of square-ended transepts. There is a mosaic 'of a bold chequer pattern' in the apse (like everything else at Silchester it is, of course, once again hidden by the soil) and it has been suggested that the altar stood at this point of intersection of nave, apse and transepts. Traces of red tessellation have been found in the nave and elsewhere, and on the evidence of coins still sticking to the original floor mass of lime and mortar, it is clear that the church cannot have been built before 360, that is, nearly fifty years after the promulgation of the Edict for the Toleration of the Christians by Constantine the Great in AD 313.

The officiating priest would have stood behind the altar, facing east, with the choir in the nave, and the worshippers kneeling and standing behind, and in the aisles. The converts, those who had not been baptised, the catechumens, stood in the narthex, watching the Christian mysteries through the doors. A Syrian document of the eighth century states that after the gifts for the Eucharist had been displayed they should be taken to a place on the north (the right hand) side of the nave. That the north transept at Silchester was, in fact, cut off from the rest of the church is clearly significant. The nave walls, which would have been higher than the external aisle walls, were, no doubt, supported by columns.

In front of the church, within the atrium, the excavators found an area of concrete with a tile base of what may have been a font or a laver, with a pit serving a soakaway for the holy water to prevent its subsequent use for magical purposes. The Syrian document, quoted above, continues '. . . let there be a forecourt, and in the middle of a house for baptistery', and this demand seems to have been complied with at Silchester, albeit five centuries earlier. Comparison with the Walbrook Mithraeum shows the striking similarity of the two structures: both were basilican in form, with apsidal ends, aisles and naves. Both Christianity and Mithraism, and indeed, the worship of Isis and Dionysus, required for the initiates a closed building as opposed to the open classical type, and this secrecy was, of course, one of the prime reasons for suspicion, and ultimately the cruel persecution which the Christians had to endure. With these likenesses in mind, it will be realised that there must be a note of caution in claiming this little building as Christian. Incidentally, it is ironical that these two faiths were so close to each other in what might be called their ritualistic and architectural necessities, the one standing for loving kindness and non-resistance, the other for the stern military virtues, both contrasting sharply in their idealism with the cheerful proliferation of Gods and Goddesses (the Imperial Cult well to the fore) that sufficed for the majority. Yet, perhaps inevitably, these two cults, virtuous and austere, were violently opposed to each other. Ironically, again, it was the Christians who persecuted the Mithraists, overturned their altars and profaned their holy places: we know nothing of any retaliation.

The siting of the church is extremely interesting: here we have this tiny building of a faith that, after grievous and long drawn-out persecution, had received not only toleration but, by 360, had become politically very powerful. There was no question of this church being modestly hidden away in a side street; on the contrary it stood boldly beside the great Basilica, headquarters of the civil power, and in line with the grand entrance to the Forum where was the bronze statue of the Emperor whom all must worship. What superb arrogance! To have dared so much means that the Christians had influential support at that time, but it was a very tiny church, and that indicates clearly that they were few in number, a powerful but not popular 'minority group' as we would describe it today. In all country districts – even, it would seem, in cantonal capitals – the old faiths flourished longer than in the larger and more cosmopolitan centres such as Londinium. Here, in Calleva, this church was a forward-looking gesture, an equation (at the least) of Christ and Deified Emperor.

For a careful evaluation of this remarkable building see Chapter 14 of George C. Boon, Sichester, The Roman Town of Calleva, *1974 and Professor S. S. Frere, 'The Silchester Church'*, Archaeologia *105 (1976), 277–302. Ed. note.*

Wroxeter (Viroconium Cornoviorum)

Five years after the capture of Colchester and the submission of south-eastern Britain to the Emperor Claudius, the legions were still campaigning against their obstinate and heroic enemy Caratacus, but now in the west country, within the foothills of the Welsh mountains. Here, on the Severn, in the land of the Ordovices, he was making his last stand against the Roman governor, Ostorius Scapula, and his army. Caratacus defended a hill, rising sheer from the river, but was defeated, and fled, leaving his wife, his daughter and his brothers in the hands of the victors; the tribesmen, however, melted into the thick forests into which the Roman cavalry could not easily penetrate.

The Roman base for this decisive campaign was probably Wroxeter, where Watling Street reached the Severn. Forts and marching-camps have been found in the vicinity, and the city itself was built over military sites, but it was not until *c.* AD 56, when no doubt their hold over the south-east had been consolidated, that the Romans turned to an aggressive forward policy whose objective was the subjugation of Wales. Wroxeter – or Viroconium, to give it its ancient name – then became a legionary fortress and the headquarters of the XIVth Legion: its strength would have been approximately 6,000 men. Traces of the timber buildings and defensive ditches of this fortress have recently been discovered eight feet below the present ground level. The XIVth was withdrawn from Britain in AD 67, and its place was taken by the XXth Legion, which later served under Agricola in Scotland, and was finally transferred to Chester, which superseded Wroxeter as the most convenient base for controlling the Welsh tribes. This transfer was probably made *c.* AD 90, after the withdrawal from Scotland, and it was then that the fortress site was handed over to the civil authorities (*civitas Cornoviorum*).

At this time two other legionary fortresses, Gloucester and Lincoln, changed their active military role and became *coloniae*, but Wroxeter became the cantonal capital of the Cornovii, an unprecedented beginning for a tribal capital in Britain. This change to city state carried with it, automati-

cally, certain amenities such as Law Courts and Forum, large public baths, drainage and water supply, and the local squirearchy would gravitate towards it and build large town houses, as happened until comparatively recently in our county towns. We have little information about the history or development of Wroxeter, but what there is indicates that it was by the end of the second century a place of wealth and importance, though its beginnings would not seem to have been particularly propitious. Military establishments great and small always attracted civil populations, tradesmen and shopkeepers, and hangers-on of all kinds, and such people, together with retired legionaries, would have formed the nucleus of the new town of Viroconium. Dr Graham Webster has pointed out that the Legion's retirement rate would have been between 180 and 200 men per annum, and that it is likely that a high proportion of them would have married local women and remained near their base, serving their old comrades by setting up shops and businesses of all kinds.

Viroconium was a very large town, of almost 200 acres within its defences, and measuring 4,000 feet from north to south and 3,000 feet from east to west, shaped like a very angular pear with the Severn flowing along its west side, and a tributary stream, the Bell Brook, with deeply shelving banks flowing through its northern section. Air photographs have produced evidence of a concentration of timber buildings in this northern area, leaving the much larger southern part of this city for more substantial and important structures, including the administrative buildings and the baths.

HOUSES AND TEMPLE
The drawing shows some of these large structures, including a somewhat mysterious stadium-like enclosure, between whose double line of walls may once have been banks of wooden seats for spectators of whatever events took place there. Unfortunately, it has not been possible to excavate more than a portion of this construction because of the

intrusion of a modern road, and erosion caused by the River Severn, which can be very turbulent in the winter. The houses, shops and temple flanked the main street of Viroconium, and the traveller coming from the north passed the Basilica and Forum on the right, and the Public Baths on the left. Four hundred feet ahead the road takes a sharp turn to the right and diverges to the town-gate and the bridge over the river, and in the distance it can be seen aimed at the gap in the Church Stretton hills. The buildings in the foreground were shops with living quarters at the rear, but the large building with the two courtyards, and hypocausts, and an arcade facing the street, which may have sheltered shops, was perhaps a priest's house linked with the adjoining temple.

Building and rebuilding continued through the centuries on this site, and coin evidence indicates occupation from *c.* AD 105 to *c.* 380. Fragments of painted wall-decoration and mosaic have been found, as well as many precious small objects, all showing that wealth and even luxury were not inconsistent with the priestly life. Along the side of the street ran a water main with the flow of water regulated by an ingenious series of sluices, whereby water could be diverted into channels under the houses. In the building described above, a channel led from the main, skirted the courtyard, flushed the latrine, went under the stadium and finally discharged into the river seven hundred feet to the west. The temple and its associated buildings were erected after an extensive fire in the mid-second century, when many timber buildings along the street were destroyed. It appears to have been of the usual Romano-Celtic type, with a nearly square high *cella* surrounded by a portico with a lean-to roof, and set in an arcaded courtyard. There is some evidence from a piece of sculpture that it may have been linked with a horse cult, and it is interesting to speculate on what possible connection there may have been between the temple and the nearby stadium, where it is reasonable to think displays involving horses may have taken place. The temple was stripped of statues and furnishings in the early

fourth century, and this may have been the work of Christians inclined more to fanaticism than charity, who saw in this religious complex of temple, priests' house, bath-house for ritual bathing and shops for souvenir votive objects, a fitting target for their intolerant violence.

THE BATHS

This great bath complex occupied an entire *insula*, measuring 290 by 440 feet, in a central position in the Roman city, adjacent to the Basilica and Forum, but separated from them by the main street linking the north and south town-gates. The basilican-type hall, on the northern side of this Baths *insula* and aligned east and west, was long thought to be the actual Basilica, or Law courts, until in 1935 Dr Kathleen Kenyon suggested that, though originally intended to be part of the usual basilica-and-forum complex of law-courts,

administrative centre and place of assembly which were to be found in all Roman towns of any size, it was left unfinished and derelict. Then, *c.* A D 160 (so it was argued), it was completed but its function was changed, and the great aisled hall became the *palaestra* or exercise hall of the grandiose bath establishment which began to come into use at that time. To complicate the matter still further, it has also been suggested that for a period prior to its conversion to *palaestra*, it may have served as part of an official residence. Meanwhile, on the site west of the *palaestra*, on the other side of the street, a Basilica and Forum were at last built (*c.* 129) superseding a Bath-house begun at the end of the first century – and never finished! This excessively complicated series of building operations, hesitating, infirm of purpose, weakly extravagant, is not at all the popular idea of the Roman character, which we prefer to think of as firm,

orderly, and above all, notable for strong common sense. This *palaestra* is remarkable for its being roofed, for when the Romans imported into Britain their conception of the 'bath-suite' they made no concession to the British climate, so much less genial than that of the Mediterranean lands to which they were accustomed, so exercise-yards were left open to the sky. Later, however, though admittedly in only a few instances known to us, *palaestrae* were roofed, and Wroxeter is important evidence of this early victory of the British climate over the intruding foreigner with his new ideas. But it must be admitted that at Wroxeter, where there is so much inconclusive attribution of purpose, the roof may well have been in existence at an early date.

The central entrance to the baths leads from the road west of the complex, between a small colonnaded market with shops and store-rooms on three sides, and a range of

The Hadrianic inscription from the Forum at Wroxeter

buildings including a large latrine, into an open colonnaded space with an ornamental pool (*piscina*) which also led to a door in the south side of the *palaestra*; the main public entrance to the baths was through the west wall of the *palaestra*. At the eastern end of the great exercise hall were changing rooms with lockers, and from floor sweepings and animal bones which have been found by excavators, it would seem that eating – and presumably drinking – was included in the entertainment offered by the establishment. Large double-doors opened into the *frigidarium* (or cold room) which was provided with two cold plunge baths where the bathers would cool themselves after the games and exercises in the *palaestra*. From the *frigidarium* the bather could go into the *laconica*, two rooms of differing temperatures of dry heat, or the *tepidarium*, wet, tepid heat, which led to the *caldarium*, or hot room, at the south end of this massively vaulted bath block. Heat was supplied by hot air rising through wall-flues from furnace heat which circulated beneath the floors. Water was piped into a boiler above the furnace beneath the south end of the *caldarium*. The supply came in by an aqueduct, leading to a special baths supply, perhaps of hollowed timber pipes connected with iron collars. The aqueduct entered the town north east of the baths, and while outside the town was in the form of an open channel. From the *caldarium* boiler hot water was fed to two large tanks in the projections on each side of the room.

Soon after this enormous block had been built its sheer weight caused it to settle in the soft sandy subsoil in spite of its massive foundations going down twelve feet below ground level. It was decided to prevent further trouble by constructing a retaining wall round three sides. This is five feet thick at ground level and increases in width below this by offsets, and it was taken to the base of the original wall. This retaining wall was built only to a height of six feet above ground level then finished flush with a mortar capping. What is interesting is that this wall has survived while the main walls of the bath block have been totally removed by stone-robbers. The reason for this is simply that this wall stood above the ground after the final collapse of the building, and attracted the attention of those looking for dressed stones; they took it down and followed it into the ground quite oblivious of the fact that there was another wall outside it, the top of which was more deeply buried and out of sight. So we can study the missing walls from their reverse 'image' in the walls built against them.

In addition to the great bath-suite there was a smaller one at right angles to it entered from the *frigidarium*. We know when this was added since its construction changed the whole character of the colonnaded court round the *piscina* by cutting off access for the *palaestra*. So the colonnades and pool were dismantled and the latter filled in with domestic town rubbish, each daily or weekly load being sealed with a clean layer of sand to prevent it becoming a stinking nuisance. This large deposit contained masses of broken pottery and they indicate that the change of plan took place *c*. 210. The central entry and colonnaded walks became service corridors except for access to the latrine which was now detached from the *palaestra*, and maybe a door was knocked through its south wall – but damage to the wall at this point has removed any evidence.

The *piscina* is the most remarkable discovery at the Wroxeter baths – it was an open air pool, as yet unique in Britain, but it is a provincial, faraway echo of the arcaded Canopus canal at Hadrian's Villa at Tivoli.

The baths ceased to function *c*. 300, and the building was probably converted into tenements in the fourth century. The great Basilican hall (*palaestra*) on the north side was totally demolished, and large timber buildings were erected on the site. How it came about that the massive fragment of the south wall of this great structure should have survived is referred to by Dr Graham Webster as 'the miraculous preservation above ground of a length of walling . . . one of the only three substantial portions of walls of Roman civil buildings in Britain which have survived the stone robbers of medieval and later times'. It is interesting that two of these formed the end wall of the *frigidarium*, the other being the Jewry Wall at Leicester. It has stood for centuries in the midst of cornfields, and has been known for hundreds of years as 'The Old Work'.

Caerwent (Venta Silurum)

This Roman town, Venta Silurum, in South Wales is interesting and important because it has the finest visible stretch of wall and bastions in Britain, still standing to an impressive height. It is also one of those few towns which are not buried under medieval and later houses; although there is a village in the centre round the church, there are still large open spaces. Some of these have been excavated, but there are opportunities here for much more work and study, as well as for opening up the remains for public enjoyment. In short, the potentialities of this little town are very great.

It may seem ironic that this apparently peaceful and flourishing settlement should develop as the capital of the Silures, the most hostile tribe the Roman army had to face. One Roman governor, Ostorius Scapula, became so enraged and embittered by his struggle against these tough warriors, that he swore to exterminate the whole tribe! After such an inauspicious start, it says much for the Roman patience and diplomacy that, two or three generations later, these people accepted the Roman way of life. This may have happened somewhere in the early second century when peace had become firmly established perhaps through a decision by the emperor Hadrian, and the earlier pottery found in the town most likely belongs to an auxiliary fort planted here in the first century, when the situation was so different.

Excavations here so far have not produced a firm date of establishment of this town, but there is a dedication in the Newport Museum which formed the base of a statue dated to the year A D 152. This is a civil inscription referring to a guild in the town and it means that the town must have been a going concern by then. The dedication is also of interest, since it links the several deities Mars Lenus with Ocelus Vellaunus. Lenus was a deity peculiar to Trier and Vellaunus associated with Mercury by a German tribe, the Allobroges. There is also an altar to Mars Lenus put up by a serving soldier of the rank of *optio*, who came under the centurion. Some of the inhabitants were Germans, introduced either through the army or by trade.

This second inscription can be seen in the church porch together with another, which is more important being one of the few which throw any light on the tribal government in Britain. This fine stone is a dedication to a patron of the town, Tiberius Claudius Paulinus, who had been the commander of *Legio II Augusta* at nearby Carleon, and who also was later to become the governor of lower Britain. The tribe thus secured a powerful friend, a little before AD 220. The inscription states in its closing line, that it was put up by a decree of the tribal senate (*ex decreto ordinis respublica civitas Silurum*).

In the centre of the town stood the Forum with its Basilica excavated in 1907–9, but back-filled; it is of the normal pattern, except that a small temple has been inserted into the west range of shops round the courtyard. To the east of the Forum there was a religious establishment, which is thought to have included a priest's house, shops selling votive objects, and of course the temple itself, which was the only part of this site which was not filled in and so can now be seen. There are other visible remains inside the town consisting of a row of houses along a Roman side street in Pound Lane, and which were excavated in 1947–8. The site was found to have a complicated history so the visitor may find the maze of walls difficult to understand. The houses began as simple rectangular strips with the narrow axis at right angles to the street and had shops at the front with living room and storage space at the back. About the middle of the second century extensions were built and later two of the shops were amalgamated into a single property, and it was developed into a courtyard-type house, with an imposing colonnade front projecting some ten feet into the street. The house next door began as one of this developed type, but only part of it has been exposed. Both houses had heated rooms with tessellated pavements. By the end of the fourth century, these five houses were in a state of decay with their inhabitants digging holes in the pavements and pulling down some of the walls, which clearly indicates this kind of decline into barbarism found elsewhere in the

Province. Extensive excavations were carried out from 1899 until 1913 and although they are not very informative about the history of the site, they did at least recover the plans of houses in the south-west area of the town. Work elsewhere has produced a large *mansio* or inn at the south gate, part of a bath-house opposite the Forum near the centre and, in the north-east quarter, a structure which has been described as an amphitheatre. This did not, however, have banked seating but was merely an oval enclosure with a little wall round it. This structure came later in the history of the town, since houses had been demolished to accommodate it: the function of such an arena could have been primarily religious, but used also for sport.

The real glory of Caerwent is its walls and bastions on the west and south sides which are worth going a long way to see. An earth bank was put up at the end of the second century and the stonework added later, probably in two stages. Excavations on the bastions produced coins from under the floors, showing that they could not have been built before 330 and they could be as late as Theodosius. The wall itself may belong to the third century, and an interesting detail is the provision of internal projections or counterforts at about 200 feet thought to be for stairways to the top of the rampart. There are substantial remains of the south gate, a single arch 'opening' almost 9 feet wide, although part was dismantled when the gate was blocked up late in the history of the town, a stone drain can be seen below the road and it was raised when the opening was blocked. A similar gate on the north side can be seen in the yard of the North Gate Inn. This gate was a single arched opening, but the stone blocks with the iron sockets for the wood gate, are only just under 5 feet from the top of the arch. This is due to the gradual building up of the road, which must originally have been at least 2 feet lower. The blocking was made when the gate was already in a ruined condition: it left a narrow opening by the east pier. The lintel of this late opening is a piece of cornice moulding which must have been taken from a building or tomb

monument. There are fragments of the two other gates on the east and west sides also visible. An interesting relic of a later age is the Norman motte which was built into the south-east angle of the town defences, a very suitable site with substantial protection on two sides. Many of the finds from the excavations in the town can be seen in the Museum at Newport.

Bath (Aquae Sulis)

Bath, or Aquae Sulis, has been described as the 'most sophisticated town in Roman Britain', and this quality of sophistication was the result of the attractive power of the hot springs with their medicinal properties. In the Roman world of the second and third centuries fashionable society came to Aquae Sulis to be cured of real or fancied ills, just as it did in the eighteenth and nineteenth centuries. There was, however, one important difference: visitors who went to Aquae Sulis not only bathed in the sacred waters but worshipped in the temple of the presiding deity Sulis Minerva: in the Bath of Beau Nash the waters were certainly not looked upon as sacred, and one might say that the temperature of religion, unlike that of the sacred spring, had fallen considerably. The British god Sul (Romanised as Sulis) was equated with the goddess Minerva, and this mingling of masculine and feminine is expressed in the fiercely moustachioed Gorgon's head which has miraculously survived from the pediment of the temple.

It is probable that there was an Iron Age, or even Bronze Age shrine on the site, and although Sul in Celtic mythology may have been connected with sun-worship rather than with the sacred spring (which even today gushes out a third of a million gallons of mineral water daily at a temperature of 50°C.), it is unlikely that such an extraordinary phenomenon would have been unnoticed or unrevered in pre-Roman days. The Romans, of course, quickly realised its potentialities. But the importance of Aquae Sulis was not entirely due to its hot springs, for there was an important crossing of the River Avon at that point, and it is likely that Aulus Plautius built a fort on the site when he was campaigning in the west towards the Fosse Way as early as AD 44–5. The level platform of land commanding the ford, and three quarters surrounded by the curving river, was in fact an ideal tactical site, though finally the town decayed because of the flooding to which it became increasingly liable. Aquae Sulis was an important road junction, and was connected with the south coast ports, through which came thousands of patients and pleasure seekers from the main-

land of Europe: Abonae (Sea Mills) to the north-west linked the spa with South Wales by a ferry across the River Severn, so that the great fortress of Caerleon and the town at Caerwent became easily accessible.

Aquae Sulis was never a large town, and only 23 acres lay within the defensive works, which were probably in being by the end of the second century. But it was, apart from the Temple Baths, an important market centre, and an indication of the richness of the locality may be deduced from the fact that the remains of no less than thirty villas have been discovered within a ten-mile radius. The Great Temple and Baths establishment and probably a theatre to the east of it, occupied the exact centre of the walled area and the greater part of it, and the modern streets preserve a ghost of the Roman street plan. Two lesser bathing establishments, though still monumental in scale, served the needs of the visitors, who squeezed into the lodging houses and inns which must have been a special feature of this unique town. These smaller bath complexes were also built over hot springs: the one is now known as the Hot Bath and the other as the Cross Bath – they lie south-west and north-west of the Great Bath. Aquae Sulis developed rapidly in the first century AD. This was the age of the Flavians, when doubt and pessimism were unknown in the Roman world and vigorous advance was the keynote to life, and this continuous development is demonstrated in the town by the extensions and rebuildings in the Great Baths and the structures associated with it.

Then, in the late third and early fourth centuries, there is evidence of change, and it would seem that open sites within the defences began to be packed with new buildings, a stone wall was built to strengthen the earlier earth rampart – the wealthy villa owners began to move into the town for security. With Irish pirates raiding up the Bristol Channel and the Severn, and Saxon pirates making the English Channel unsafe, the stream of visitors from overseas may have dried up. British roads and the countryside were at times hazardous for the traveller too, but sea pirates and

land brigands were not responsible for this decline of the Bath Spa. The real culprit was a recession climate which led to a dramatic rise in the water table and in the third and fourth centuries the hypocausts were continually flooded. Then the floors were raised, but eventually rising flood waters had led to the massive foundations being weakened and serious structural faults developed, which culminated in the abandonment of the great buildings, and the enormous vaults collapsed into what had become a marsh, into which the famous spring was still pouring its hot radioactive waters. But still the town survived in some prosperity, and even in the early fifth century substantial stone houses were being built on the slightly higher ground. A blow to the Britons of Aquae Sulis was struck in 577, when the Saxons defeated their forces at the Battle of Dyrham, but the site continued to be occupied and it was the scene in 973 of the coronation of King Edgar.

THE BATH COMPLEX

The drawing shows the Baths in their final form, and though later various internal alterations were made, they did not significantly alter the external appearance of the great complex. When first built the baths were probably roofed with tiles, supported by a timber structure similar to the normal basilican pattern with aisles at a lower level, but soon the impregnated steam from the hot thermal water began to twist the beams and endanger their stability. So a series of massive masonry vaults were constructed, and, although box tiles were used, all the supporting walls and columns had to be strengthened to support the increased load. The Baths were not built directly over the hot spring, which was contained in a pool roughly octagonal in shape adjacent to the long north wall of the main block. This octagon was later enclosed by a massive buttressed wall, which supported a huge vault – one of the several subsidiary to the main vault covering the Great Bath. The very hot spring water was led through a lead box-pipe into the Great Bath, where it cooled sufficiently for bathing. An elaborate

drainage system with its outlet into the River Avon has been discovered, much of it intact, and part of it in use today. The Great Bath was a swimming bath, but at both ends of the main block there were suites of hot, tepid and cold baths of the conventional Roman type, and there was also at the east end a tepid bath fed from the Great Bath, and presumably of a lower temperature, whilst at the west end was the Circular Cold Bath, tightly set in a lofty square compartment. The two conventional suites, served by supplies of non-thermal water, were extravagant facilities for male and female bathers, each with their *caldarium*, *tepidarium*, *frigidarium*, with hypocausts and independent stoking arrangements. One can marvel that this great establishment, constantly in use in what must have been a high state of efficiency, with enlargements and improvements being made until a late date, should have survived intact for at least three hundred years – which is equivalent in time to the period between the reigns of Queen Elizabeth I and Queen Elizabeth II.

Immediately to the north, and in exact alignment with the Baths, was the Temple of Sulis Minerva set in its colonnaded precinct, and, although its dedication was Celtic as well as Roman, the architectural form was wholly classical. The temple stood on a podium measuring 33 by 67 feet, and the many carved fragments found since 1790 have made possible a rational reconstruction. There were four fluted Corinthian columns and a portico two columns deep at the east end, and a *cella* with five attached columns occupying the whole width of the podium: it has been compared with the Temple of Fortuna Virilis in Rome. The pediment was ornamented with the fiercely moustachioed Gorgon's Head mentioned above, held aloft by victories in the form of winged female figures, with tritons blowing conches, or horns, at each end: it is a curious mixture of the splendidly barbarian Celtic art of Britain with the partly assimilated figurative art of Mediterranean culture. The precinct (or, more properly, *temenos*) was entered from the eastern end through a two-arched monumental gateway, and the visitor would have been confronted by an altar, twenty feet wide,

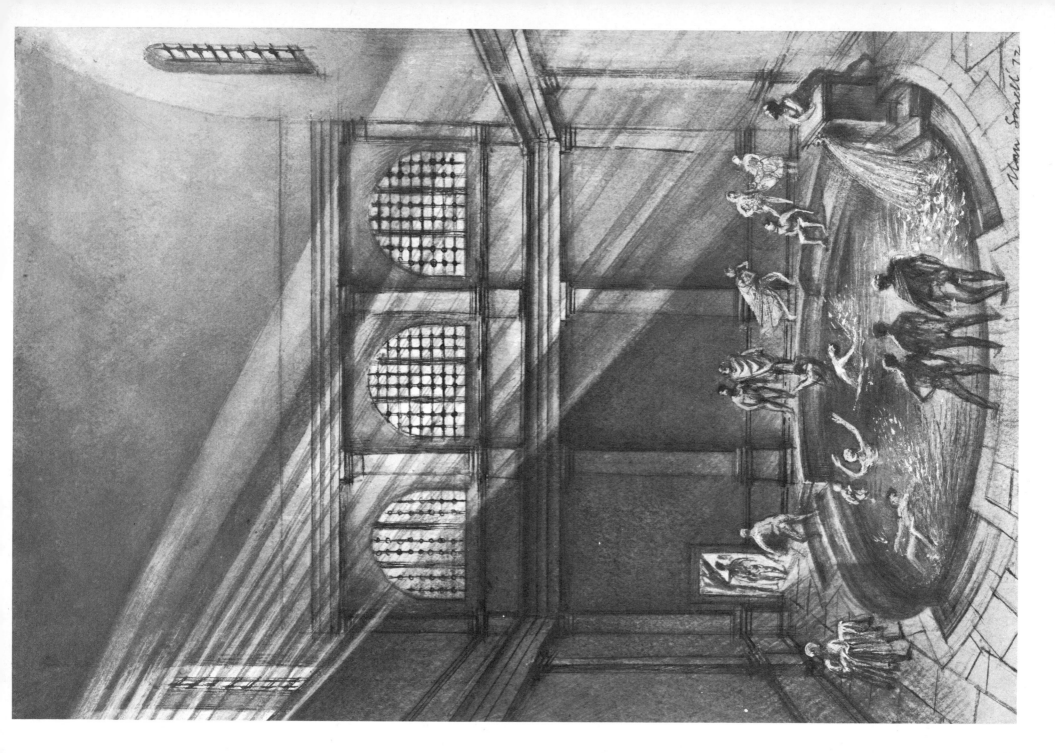

and, of course, the east facade of the temple beyond. The temple and this altar were further protected from the casual promenaders by an inner free-standing colonnade. On the left of the gateway was the immense bulk of the Baths, and between the buttresses which took the thrust of the vault over the spring and reservoir it is reasonable to think there stood a structure with a central doorway, known to us as the Facade of the Four Seasons, and it has been suggested that the Luna Pediment, so-called from the three fragments found in 1790, may have surmounted the facade. The doorway might well have formed the entrance to the vaulted area, where, it is supposed, an observation platform supported by columns was situated.

The conjunction of religion, sacred spring with its steamy gush, medicinal and all the luxury of the hot and cold bath suites, and the sheltered colonnades, must have formed an attractive combination, but added to all these it is very likely that the substantial remains which have been noted to the east of the temple precinct are those of a theatre. Comparison with similar continental sites reinforces this supposition – so here in Aquae Sulis we have every reason to suppose there was a centre catering for a very wide range of human needs and desires – and in magnificent style: it was one of the largest spa-baths in the Roman Empire.

We know little enough of the town surrounding the Baths, because it has been submerged by the modern city, and much of the medieval and Georgian architecture is sacrosanct, but discoveries have been made and amongst them, in 1869, were several fragments of a 'gigantic cornice' twice the size of the Temple cornice: there is no clue as to where the building stood, or what it was.

THE CIRCULAR OR COLD BATH
The Circular Bath, which is also known as the Cold Bath, has a diameter of 28 feet. It did not form part of the original architectural scheme, and this becomes obvious when it is seen how awkwardly it was squeezed into what had earlier been either a fine entrance hall or, perhaps, a dressing room with open arcades at the north and south ends. When the Circular Bath was added, these arcades were filled in, and the remaining central area became square in plan. Later, it became necessary to re-roof the baths, and column-buttresses were added to give additional support to the east and west walls. The Circular Bath had no connection, of course, with the thermal spring, and the cold water came from a 'fountain-like structure' on the north side of the bath. The door shown in the drawing led into the *tepidarium*, and the shock of the cold plunge came after the enervation of the hot rooms. The Circular Bath was lined with lead sheeting, as were all the other baths, and some idea of the great quantities of lead used may be gained when we learn that a certain Major Davis, City Engineer in the nineteenth century, when engaged in building the modern baths on the site, wrenched up, and subsequently sold, 30 tons of Roman lead sheeting from the floor of the Great Bath.

Caister-on-Sea (Venta Icenorum)

There are two Caisters in Norfolk, and although Caister-on-Sea and Caistor St Edmunds, two miles south of Norwich, are in no way connected, in Roman times they were important links in the chain which bound the Province into an economic whole. Caister St Edmunds was Venta Icenorum, the cantonal capital of the Iceni, who inhabited what is today Norfolk and north-west Suffolk. East Anglia has always had a remoteness not at all related to its geographical position, and the Iceni were not involved in resistance to the Claudian invasion: they made terms with the invaders and ranked as an ally, or client kingdom. However, Boudicca more than redressed the balance when in AD 60, her revolt nearly overthrew the Roman rule. The inevitable Roman counterblow began with a policy of ruthless and vindictive revenge, but this was quickly reversed by the intervention of Julius Classicianus, the newly appointed Procurator, who, fortunately for the Iceni, arrived in Britain at this time. All the evidence, such as it is, points to a less than average degree of Romanisation in the lands of the Iceni, and this surely means that they were left to themselves and not made to suffer too severely for their desperate but ill-timed attempt to reverse an inevitable process of change. It is significant that the road system seems to have been remarkably underdeveloped in the canton compared with the coherent network which criss-crossed the other parts of the Province.

Venta Icenorum, unlike the majority of Roman foundations, was not sited on a river-bank, and consequently trade-goods could not reach it as they did Colchester or London, or many inland towns such as St Albans or York. A sea-port, to serve the cantonal capital and its hinterland, therefore, soon became necessary, and Caister-on-Sea, as we know it today, was founded, on slightly rising land to the north of what in Roman times was a great estuary formed by the river Waveney, Yare and Bure. A road from Venta Icenorum has been traced north-east to the Yare – then the Gariannus – and no doubt it continued across the river to link up with the road which emerged from the west gate of Caister-on-Sea. It will be noticed that the mouth of the Rhine lies due east of the Norfolk coast, and since a considerable volume of trade came from the Rhine to Britain it will be realised that a port sited in the Caister locality would be economically very profitable, not only for the canton of the Iceni, but also for the British heartland to the west. We do not know whether Caister drew off any appreciable amount of trade from Colchester or London, but the fact that there was this Norfolk port, with its quay and sheltered deep water anchorage, must have been attractive to the masters of the clumsy merchant-ships of those times, especially when they realised that here was a haven which could be reached without any difficult tortuous river navigation. It is interesting to note that from the Hook of Holland to Caister is 110 miles, compared with 145 miles to Colchester and 185 to London, so that Caister had a distinct (and rather surprising advantage) over both these ports.

Proof of the success of the new town has come to light in the excavations which commenced in 1951 under the direction of the late Charles Green. It became evident that the town in its earliest form, and dated to the first half of the second century AD, was square in plan, each side measuring about 450 feet, with timber fortifications and a single ditch. The value and importance of the new town must have been quickly recognised, for by the middle of the century it was extended to a square measuring 590 feet, and a substantial defensive wall was built: it was 10 feet thick, flint-faced with brick courses, and was pierced by four single-arched gates, each with twin towers. There was also an internal corner tower at the south-east angle – though to speak of 'angles' in this context is incorrect, as the corners were all rounded as in all military works of the period. Indeed, the military lay-out, shape and general character is remarkable in this second phase of Caister. The wall enclosed seven and a half acres, but the entire occupied area, excluding the space between the South Gate and the estuary, may have been as much as 30 acres. Just inside this gate a large building of the late second century has been discovered: it has been variously described as a seamen's hostel or a meeting place for visiting merchants. Careful excavation has shown that it was repaired from time to time, and that in c. 340 the so-called 'tap-room' was destroyed by fire, and not rebuilt, though the rest of the building remained in occupation.

There was a road paved with beach cobbles, with sidewalks, leading from the South Gate to the quay, which, projecting boldly into the estuary, protected the Inner Basin on its west flank. On its east flank was a boat-basin with a cobbled hard where small craft could be hauled up for repair – one can imagine the local fishing fleet using this basin. Pottery kilns have been found south-west of the town, and there is thought to have been a 'shanty town' outside the North Gate.

Towards the end of the third century a great fortress, with a naval dockyard and harbour, was built on the opposite shore of the estuary, five miles south of Caister, and was known to the Romans as Gariannonum and to us as Burgh Castle. This was part of the massive coastal defence scheme – the Saxon Shore Forts – along the east and south coasts of Britain (and the north and west coasts of Gaul) to protect the provinces which were being assailed by the ever-increasing barbarian raids from across the North Sea. The construction of these great fortresses was, in fact, a sign of weakness rather than strength, though it probably had a short term effectiveness. It was at this time that the Caister defensive ditch system was extended. Originally, the single ditch had been dug outside the palisade, but when the flint wall was built and sited some feet inside the palisade, the early ditch was filled in, and a second was dug nearer to the wall. A third ditch was then dug outside the early one, but overlapping in places, and only small adjustments were made thereafter. The town still prospered in the third and fourth centuries, but gradually, with the province beginning to disintegrate, and overseas trade becoming precarious and then dwindling to virtual extinction, Caister, its purpose gone, declined and died.

Caister-on-Sea: a panoramic view of the Venta Icenorum

The civil settlements attached to the forts

The areas of civil life which are sometimes overlooked by the students of Roman Britain, are those in the military zones. These are the communities which lived outside the gates of the forts. Soldiers have basic needs the world over and at all times throughout history, when they pile out of the barracks in off duty times, they need to add to their military diet by more tasty and exotic foods. They consume vast quantities of alcohol and most of them also want women. It is easy to see how these requirements were met and a kind of shanty village would spring up overnight as soon as the troops settled in. What may be more difficult to understand is how such an unsavoury beginning could lead to a small town with substantial permanent buildings. The answer is the length of occupation; some of these forts were held for several hundred years – plenty of time for growth and development. This was helped by the practice of many soldiers staying near their base when they retired. They had often spent most of their life in the same fort, they were recruited quite young, at 15 and 16 sometimes, and would have lost any connections with their homeland. The thrills of the ale houses and brothels were soon displaced by the need for home and family, so many of them had already a place in the community and they stayed there to be with their old comrades, and there was nowhere else to go. As the size of the community grew, so it in turn attracted shop-keepers, traders and skilled craftsmen.

Every fort in Britain would have had its civil settlement even those on the northernmost frontier, the Antonine Wall, which was held for less than thirty years. An inscription near the fort at the east end of this Wall refers to the *vicani Veluniati*. The term *vicus* was used for settlements of all sizes wherever they were, unless they had a higher municipal status and the *vicani* were the inhabitants. From Auchendavy, another fort on the Antonine Wall, came the tombstone of a youth called Salmanes, maybe from a family of Semitic traders, on the other hand, they could have been servants of an officer. We are on much surer ground on Hadrian's Wall, where there is ample evidence of quite large settlements and one of the best known is that at Housesteads. Much of the information has come from air photographs which show up the slight bumps and hollows in the ground, especially, when after a light snowfall. It is one of the few northern settlements to be excavated and four seasons' digging in 1931–4 uncovered an area of small rectangular houses just outside the south gate to the fort, flourishing in the third and fourth centuries. The earlier *vicus* is probably to the south of this beyond the *vallum* which was the military boundary to the Wall in the second century, but the changes in the army introduced by Severus, including the legality of soldiers' marriages, led to the *vallum* going out of use and from then on civil buildings spread over it up to the very walls of the fort. This late development also can be seen on air photo-graphs published by Professor J. K. St Joseph, which shows at least 11 acres of buildings to the west of the fort, sheltering under the great Wall itself, and there are indications of another but much smaller spread on the east side. Surface evidence of the second century *vicus* has been obliterated by later ploughing, but the lack of adequate drainage in the site became buried under peat; this will have the effect of preserving much of the wood, textiles and leather, so that excavation will one day produce some very rich deposits, as they have already done at Chesterholm. Earlier finds indicate the presence of at least seven temples and there has been an interesting series of altars. These include one to a triad of German deities, the Alaisiagae, Baudihillia and Friagabis and another to two Alaisiagae, Beda and Fimmilena, which suggests that the period of greatest prosperity was in the third and fourth centuries.

These are only two examples of this type of settlement which happen to have been studied more extensively than any others; in some areas like Wales hardly any work has been done on it at all. But it must not be forgotten that there were civilians living outside all the forts and that in most cases they continued to do so when the army moved on; thus, most of the towns of Roman Britain owed their beginnings to the presence of troops. Eventually, we must hope that much more attention will be paid to these *vici*, since they are obviously a very important element in the life of the military areas, especially in the late period and they will have much to offer in our understanding of the processes of the degradation of Romanised culture under increasing barbarian influence.

CORBRIDGE: TEMPLES AND MILITARY ENCLOSURES
The two irregular fortified enclosures on the left were occupied by legionary craftsmen, armourers and the like, who supplied the garrison of the Wall with equipment and stores. The irregularity of their plan was due to the small road-side temples of an earlier date, which could not be encroached upon.

The two square courtyard buildings inside the nearer compound were officers' houses; the other buildings in both compounds were either workshops or soldiers' quarters, with the exception of two buildings in the foreground, both with apsidal ends, and these were *scholae* – club rooms and shrines for the use of NCOs and men in their off-duty hours.

The long range of buildings on the other side of the Stanegate, part of the great storehouse left unfinished at the death of Severus, was later probably divided into shops to serve the thriving town.

At the far end of this massive fragment was a fountain, the water discharging into a cistern, and thence into an oblong tank. It was ornamented with statues on pedestals. Beyond the fountain were two externally buttressed granaries with a system of air circulation beneath the raised floors, so that the stored grain could be kept dry.

HOUSESTEADS CIVIL SETTLEMENT
The road shown in the drawing was paved with flag-stones, and it had a paved sidewalk. The houses flanking it were of the usual narrow rectangular shape, end-on to the street, often terminating in open-fronted shops. The lower storeys were constructed of the local stone, and the upper were

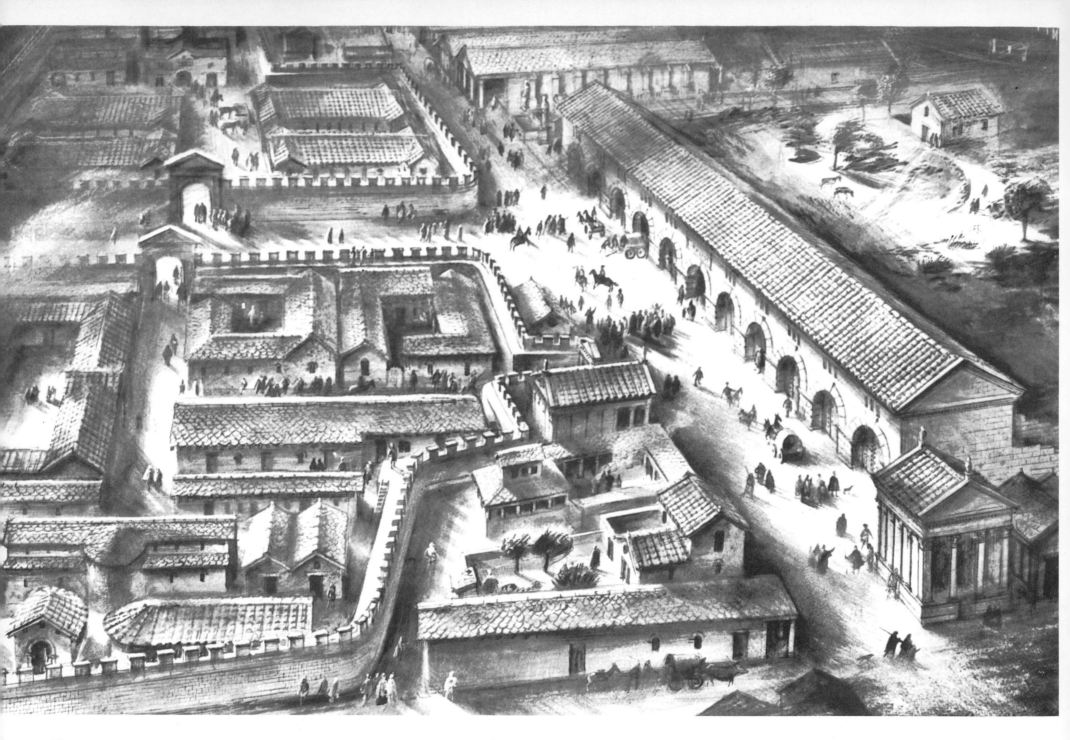

THE CIVIL SETTLEMENTS ATTACHED TO THE FORTS

Corbridge Roman Station, third century AD

timber-framed, very like surviving medieval dwellings. Another road, or lane, debouched from the fort gate to the left at a sharp angle, and a house built of fine masonry had its corner adapted to this angle. The lane connected Housesteads with Chesterholm, or Vindolanda, a fort on the Stanegate.

The hillside where the settlement stood was terraced, and here were kitchen gardens, or perhaps patches of struggling wheat. Seven or eight temples, including a Mithraeum, served the religious needs of the people, and in addition there were several smaller shrines.

Housesteads Civil Settlement, fourth century AD

Next page
Relief of Mithras from Housesteads

Index

Figures in **heavy type** denote pages on which illustrations appear.